The Sea Trout Diaries

R.W. Mountjoy

This collection of notes and photographs is dedicated to the past and present members of the Tavy, Walkham and Plym Fishing Club who created and have maintained the second oldest fishing association in England.

First published in 2007 by
The Crapstone Press
12 Morley Drive
Crapstone
Yelverton
Devon PL20 7UY

Copyright R.W. Mountjoy 2007

ISBN 978-0-9555979-0-9

Contents

My thanks to my wife Sian and daughters Kirry and Rebecca for proof reading the copy and taking some of the photographs.

Introduction

The Specialist

The sea trout is a very special fish. It is mysterious, elusive, hard to catch, delicious to eat and totally wild. I have tried and enjoyed many forms of angling but most of my fishing 'career' has been focused on this one species. These collected notes represent the selected and edited records of my fascination with this fish. The notes contain some theories about sea trout, theories that have influenced the ways I have set out to pursue them. I do not profess to be an expert – the sea trout continues to confound me and constantly remind me of the limits of my skill and knowledge, but that is one of its attractions.

I have aspired to gain sufficient skill to be able to pick my time and place and take a brace on my terms. Alas, the sea trout do not play my game and when I think I have just about cracked it the rules seem to change and I have to rethink my tactics. But this is the joy of fishing – you never really know what is happening under the surface of the water or what will respond to the next cast. In publishing these notes I hope to help the angler who is beginning to discover the merits of this very special species and perhaps, to encourage debate amongst those well versed.

There have been some excellent books written on sea trout fishing and it is not my intention to compete with any of these classics. They should be read, and the wealth of advice that they contain should be digested by anyone taking up a rod for sea trout. What I hope to do is to air some of the ideas that I have developed from many years of fishing and talking fishing with other enthusiasts. I hope that this may lead to a greater understanding of why a fish while 'programmed' not to eat, will take a lure

and how we may make this happen. This is a matter central to sea trout fishing and I believe it has not been adequately explained in other publications.

These theories and ideas have been assembled over the years, in part as a result of my own experiments and observations but much more to the advice, directions and comments of those who share my enthusiasms. On the riverbank I have watched, listened and talked with other fishermen, both ancient and modern, accepting and considering advice in equal measure. The following pages include what I have both received and discovered with comments and some deduction.

For many years now I have been privileged to live in West Devon with access to the rivers Tavy, Walkham, Plym and Meavy. I have been able to cast a line over the waters fished and written about by Major Kenneth (West Country) Dawson and Jeffrey (Sou-Wester) Bluett. I have shared beats with men and women who knew and fished with these pioneering fishing writers. The 'old timers', as I have perhaps unkindly called them, although initially cautious, have been generous to me. They have kindly shared their understanding of the sea trout and their knowledge of the rivers. I am indebted to them and thank them for their forebearance. The ideas and theories I am about to present come from the generations of fishermen and women who have loved these Devonian steams.

Most of these old timers have now left the waters and some have passed on to other beats. In fear of losing information of value to the association and those young fishermen who will follow us down the river I put

DATE	RIVER	BEAT	CONDITIONS
August 1986	Walkham	Magpie	Falling spate
NOTES			
I met one of the old-timers returning having fished the Magpie beat. The old boy, his heavy bag with the tip of a fish's tail peeping from the corner was clear that his efforts had met with success. With the hope of picking up some advice I tried to initiate some conversation. "Any luck, Mr T." I enquired to which he replied "Nope boy – nuttin about" and strode on by.			
FISH CAUGHT	0	FLY/LURE	Everything!

DATE	RIVER	BEAT	CONDITIONS
June 1989	Walkham	Magpie	
NOTES			
I fished the Magpie beat with no success and below the Viaduct Pool I met 'Tobacco Tin', one of the old-timers returning. Previously I had managed to engage him in some sort of conversation and got a few good tips. Gradually I was gaining his trust. I told him I had had no luck and he asked had I fished the 'Chip Shop'? At that time I did not know of the pool or its name. The short run under the near bank hardly met my criteria for a pool let alone a named pool. He described the pool and how to fish it "go on boy –lers a fish yerrr". And there was – my first salmon from the beat.			
FISH CAUGHT	1 salmon 7 lb	FLY/LURE	Mepp Size 4

together some fishing guides for the popular beats. These have been well received and club members have kindly suggested that I should expand it into 'a book'. Their help, support and encouragement has given me the motivation to organise and present the wisdom imparted to me and illustrate it with my own diary extracts, sketches and photographs. With the exception of those now deceased authors whose works I may refer to, I have decided to avoid identifying individuals and I will not to refer to friends, guides and mentors by their real names. I find name-dropping in publications of this kind can become tedious. I have tried to avoid tiresome fishing clichés and will try to adopt a style of prose that is direct and clear. Readers will, I hope forgive me if I lapse occasionally and present them with some over-descriptive passages, if enthusiasm gets the better of me.

The sea trout I cherish is a Celt and its UK strongholds remain at the northern and western edges of our islands. In Ireland the "white trout' have a special place in angling traditions and the Welsh have an entire sub culture focused on 'sewin', the silver one. The Principality has an ancient and now well-documented tradition of sea trout fishing. The West Country has similar customs but despite the writing of Dawson and Bluett, fishing for sea trout in the South West is to a great extent a dark and secretive activity. The magic and mystery may well have played a part in its attraction to me, but sea trout or 'peal' fishing is as deeply embedded in the culture of the South West, as it is in Ireland, Wales and the western isles of Scotland. It is an integral part of my heritage and I prize it.

Sea trout fishing is an extreme form of angling and to be consistently successful it demands the acquisition of what is best described as highly developed hunting skills. The fish is wary, extremely nervous and does its best to hide itself away from human eyes. A casual observer walking by a sea trout river on a summers

day could be forgiven for thinking the stream was devoid of fish. Apart from the rises of par and small brown trout there is very little to see in the often crystal pools. Sea trout lie motionless in the depths or secrete themselves under rocks, ledges and roots. If undisturbed they will lie in shallow runs but at the slightest movement in their 'window' their fins begin to quiver and if a shadow is cast over them they seem to dissolve. They will return, only after dark or when the river rises and darkens with peat.

Those who pursue sea trout tend to meet at night in secluded places or are up at dawn and back home before the rest of the world is up and about. They slink about and keep a low profile – not wanting to draw attention to their activities as this could result in action that would disturb the fish. Despite the perils of wild places and wild water, sea trout enthusiasts tend to operate alone. Their successes, losses and failures they keep to themselves. The catch is consumed in the company of privileged friends and family as it is far too precious to sell. Habits, rituals, methods and knowledge is held close and tight. The old-timers' I met on the rivers were always very reluctant to part with any of their secrets. Those who claimed to have caught nothing when met on the riverbank often submitted (reluctantly) seasonal returns that astounded me. Initially they resented my interest and the only insight into their methods, places and lures were discovered at first, by patience and what could be politely described as quiet observation.

Gradually persistence paid off and one by one they began to 'open up'. Once or twice I managed to catch two together and I found that if I could incite a little competition information would flow as they tried to out-do each other with stories from the 'good old days'. They began to talk of times when what would now be a good season's tally could be caught in one night. They would recount tales of great fish

taken and greater fish lost and finally when encountered on their own they began to take some pleasure in adding to my growing knowledge. One by one, looking around to see that no one else was watching they would point out an overlooked taking place or a special lie and occasionally open up a tobacco tin and give me a glimpse of a special lure.

Most of these old-timers have long gone and sadly their secrets with them. Many of the new rods on the river have moved in from 'away' and have developed as fishermen in other environments. There is a real danger that the essence of the West Country peal fishing may become lost forever. I am sure the old-timers would not want this and I share some of their secrets in the hope that they will forgive me and accept that the knowledge is being shared in the hope of keeping the traditions alive.

I grew up in North Devon amidst a clutter of distractions. I lived in Appledore some 200 yards from the river Torridge and its confluence with the Taw. A five-minute walk from our house my grandfather had a traditional clinker fishing boat moored. Between attending school in Bideford and earning pocket money from part time jobs I roamed the beaches with a fishing rod and the fields and woods with an air rifle. In those days communities were small enough and close enough for everyone to know everyone and children could wander without fear. I was subjected to benevolent neglect and as long as I returned in time for set meals I was free to go wherever. If I returned with a rabbit or a fish I was briefly a hero.

A dozen or so salmon fishing boats operated from the village in the 1960s and when I became strong enough I was occasionally offered a 'berth' - a place in the four-man crew of a salmon boat. I loved the fishing but it was extremely hard work. The heavy eighteen-foot open boat, clinker built - larch on oak, would be rowed out to a station on the estuary. This

could be several miles from the moorings and although it was invariably with the tide it was tough going. Upon reaching the allotted place the boat would be beached, the net prepared and the crew would stand ready for a jumper. Watching and waiting, two men would sit at the oars, a third stood ready to pay out the net that was stowed in the stern and the fourth on the shore with the anchor rope. No one spoke – eyes would be pealed for any movement on the water and ears cocked for any sound of a splash.

We would stand, silent and vigilant for hours at a time, the guard broken only by the need to move the boat to keep pace with the rising tide. A small group standing isolated amidst a vast plain of sand and rising water we were lost in our thoughts, our dreams and our ambitions.

A leaping fish would break the spell and all would be thrown into action. The boat would row frantically out and and attempt to encircle the fish. With the anchor rope over his shoulder and his heels dug into the beach the shore man would hold on for dear life. As the net was let out it caught the tide and threatened to snatch him off the beach and into the water. Once the boat completed its semi circle and returned to land the three would leap out to help haul in the net. Two men on the cork supported head ropes and two on the leaded foot ropes would pull together with a steady regular rhythm.

On a warm summer day with neap tides it was enjoyable, but in biting winds, driving rain or hail it was hell. There was no shelter three miles out on a flat windswept estuary and no rest from the hard back-breaking work. The net, when I was salmon fishing, was made from natural fibre – hemp and sisal - and it held hard to the water. Holding on to the shore rope when the boat was paying out on a spring tide often required a stronger man than me and at 17 years of age I was dragged down the beach and into the sea on more than one occasion. It was work I did

not do regularly and so never became 'match fit'. After fishing a tide my hands were raw with broken blisters and my back ached for days. If we were lucky and caught a salmon or two I received one fifth of the proceeds - there was traditionally one share for every man and one for the boat. I loved the open estuary and was magnetically drawn to the fishing but it was a hard living and with little material rewards

Salmon caught were taken away to be sold to the dealers but the by-catch of mullet, flounders and even bass was thrown back. It was considered unlucky to take a 'rough fish' when fishing for salmon. 'Peal or pugs', local names for sea trout, were not discarded but kept for the crew to eat themselves or barter. 'Peal' were maiden, one-winter fish that had yet to run the river and spawn. 'Pugs' were larger, heavily spotted fish that had returned to sea after spawning the previous winter and were about to make another run to the spawning beds. Once or twice each summer I would bring a peal home from fishing or one would be earned in respect of a special favour. The family would then get to dine on sea trout and it became an eagerly anticipated summer treat. The soft pink flesh that melted in the mouth was a delicacy much appreciated by everyone I knew. Salmon were best sold-on for profit but sea trout were too good for that. Sea trout were treated with great dignity – they were not sold or traded but saved for the home table or given in love and friendship.

I remember arriving home from college one holiday to find my father and my brother struggling with a large (dead) fish on the kitchen table. I expressed my pleasure at being welcomed by a banquet but my father responded with genuine disappointment, "Its only a salmon, boy – I was hoping to get you a peal!"

My grandfather was a retired sea captain who in the 1960s supplemented his pension by taking out fishing parties through the summer months. Invariably, unless occupied with school or paid employment elsewhere I was press-ganged as crew. In the summer we fished for pollack and bass with artificial eels and in the autumn we ledgered with peeler crabs for codling. As a teenager there were times when I wanted to be elsewhere but there are those steel grey dawns when the entire estuary was a vast sheet of platinum and we drew the only line across it, that remain in my memories for ever. I recall times drifting over a rising tide with no more company than an old man who often seemed impossible to please with much more affection than the days running wild with my peers.

It was a time before bass were over-exploited and they would shoal in huge numbers across the banks as the tide rose. We trolled over fish that had pushed sand eels to the surface and sailed through great flocks of cart wheeling terns. In the fresh sunshine with a steady wind on your face, the excited gulls in your ears and a good bass on a free line there was nothing better. My memories are full of fine days with a good chop on dark blue water and a pale blue sky full of white noisy sea birds. On a good summers day we could take twenty or more bass on a tide and on our return we would sell our surplus for a shilling a pound. In the 1960s there were always small hungry clusters waiting on the quay scanning the tide for returning boats. They would converge on any step or slipway as a boat was landing looking for any surplus that could be bought or scrounged. In long gabardine macs they seemed to float as they hurried to a landing, trying unsuccessfully to conceal any desperation. I quite liked sharing our bounty but it embarrassed Grandfer.

We would briefly tie up on the slip opposite the Post Office to deal with the 'gannets' (as Granfer called them) and after landing any catch and kit we would take the boat to its mooring 100 yards or so from the quay. Having secured the boat on the moorings we would get ashore

DATE	RIVER	BEAT	CONDITIONS
June 1964	Torridge (Estuary)		

NOTES

Took the boat out on the flood tide and took 8 bass to 6 lb and one small pollack on rubber eels. Hooked a large pug that I got to within sight of the boat when it took off. It was unstoppable and took out all the line and broke me. It was probably no larger than the biggest bass but fought like something else. It leapt, took off on powerful runs and charged at the boat like a demented torpedo. (At the time I had no idea that the bass were specimen fish - they were eaten with relish!)

FISH CAUGHT		FLY/LURE	

	RIVER	BEAT	CONDITIONS
August 1970	Inny		Low and clear

NOTES

Stayed at Rezarre for the weekend and we woke early to fish the little River Inny at dawn for sea trout. Spinning with light tackle was the preferred method and armed with short spinning rods, fixed spool reels and small Mepps we headed for the river. Walking upstream we covered the water in front of us casting up and across to bring the small spinner back faster than the current. We caught a couple of 'breakfast brownies' and one sea trout for supper.

FISH CAUGHT	3 brown 1 sea trout	FLY/LURE	Mepps Size 1

in a tiny home-made dingy. I never found out who built it or owned it but it was kept on a running line hitched to a bolt at the top of the slip. My grandfather would sit on the only thwart and scull over the stern while I perched precariously on the bow with my knees being knocked by Grandfer's elbows. With two of us onboard the freeboard was no more than two inches and it made for a perilous if short journey.

On one occasion an over keen 'gannet' tried to help grandfather with his catch as he alighted. He somehow lost his balance and the dingy overturned throwing him into the water. My father was miraculously on hand to leap into the water and rescue the old man as he could not swim. From then on we landed kit, catch and skipper on the slip and then I would strip to my bathing trunks to moor the boat myself and then swim ashore.

Not infrequently when fishing for bass we caught sea trout. The small school peal were hauled in without ceremony on the heavy duty hand lines we then used, but the larger 'pug' fish took some landing. Lines that had landed double-figure cod were not infrequently broken and if we did get a large sea trout to the boat it was often lost when trying to lift it over the rail. Playing a fish and netting it was viewed as frivolous by my grandfather and if we hooked a pug he could become animated with excitement but never confident of landing it. But I grew in awe of these beautiful, elusive and amazingly strong fish. On the rare occasions that he did get one in the boat it would be hidden under the canvas cover and spirited away once the boat was moored. Once home the catch that had not been sold on the quay would be cleaned in the kitchen yard and then dispersed to family friends or to those we were indebted. A sea trout would be placed on the largest plate in the house and given pride of place on the kitchen table, for that night we would dine like royalty.

Life as a child in Appledore was wonderful but sooner or later I had to grow up and earn a living. I could read, write and draw and so it looked like a precarious job in the shipyard drawing office or training to be a teacher. I chose the latter and despite having much to divert me I somehow managed to scrape the A levels to qualify.

Once I was at College, fishing was invariably limited to holidays and returns to the West Country. Fortunately I had a cousin with fishing on the river Inny in Cornwall and most summer holidays would involve a visit and a chance to fish the pretty little Tamar tributary. The river would be fished at dawn and dusk with a light spinning rod and a small spoon. Casting upstream we would catch many small brown trout and, if we were in luck, a sea trout or two.

I married and settled in Gloucestershire restricting the fishing to the occasional visit home until a teaching colleague introduced me to the art of fly-fishing. I purchased the basic tackle and after school on the football field, while detainees watched in mocking misery I was taught the rudiments of casting. Once the essentials were (almost) mastered we progressed to the water. Fortunately the little river Frome that passed through Stroud had a coarse fishing club. The Frome held some wild trout but courtesy of an upstream trout farm, a few escapees trickled down to provide free stocking. There were not that many trout but most of the members were only interested in the coarse fish. It was within walking distance of my home and cost only a few pounds a year. Over the years I caught pike, roach and chubb and a number of trout including the two largest browns I have taken. I found that brown trout taken on the gravel runs were full of fresh water shrimp and pink fleshed, almost like sea trout. Those caught over the muddy beats were pale and tasteless.

DATE	RIVER	BEAT	CONDITIONS
April 1982	Frome (Stroud)		Warn breezy – river very slight colour

NOTES

In an unusual place against the left bank a fish was steadily rising but as I approached I spooked it and it dived straight into the bank. I parted the hanging grasses to reveal a drain pipe protruding into the river and providing a steady flow to the main stream. Just inside I could see the tail of a large trout.

After about twenty minutes the fish reversed out of the drain and took up a position facing down the river but above the drain in the small eddy that the latter created. Before long it was taking flies that were being caught in the eddy created by the drain.
It took many attempts but eventually I got a cast right and the fish rose, I tightened and the fish shot up the pipe.

It was an unusual fight with a fish some ten yards up a drain pipe but eventually it was drawn out to finish the battle in the corner pool below. The beautifully spotted brown trout weighed three pounds six ounces.

FISH CAUGHT	1 brown 3lb 6oz	FLY/LURE	Greeenwell's G. Size 14

One evening in June I had an even bigger fish:

DATE	RIVER	BEAT	CONDITIONS
June 1982	Frome (Stroud)		

NOTES

It was a very warm, dry and bright evening but very windy. I was reluctant to cancel plans to spend an hour or two by the river and hoped that the valley below would be quieter. Alas it was not the case. Fish were rising but casting to them with any degree of accuracy in the blustery conditions proved impossible.

In the top section of the fishing, a drainpipe crossed the river at an oblique angle forming a small weir. Above this obstruction a fifty-yard stretch ran straight and fast beneath a bank heavy with bush alder. A large brown lived under the near bank a yard above the pipe. It lay in a quiet pocket next to the swiftest flow and was rising tonight to small dark flies.

Under normal conditions this fish was impossible to cast to. On this night the strong upstream wind allowed me to float the fly out on the breeze and between gusts drop the cast in the taking zone while holding the main line clear of the fast current. The fish rose at the first attempt but in my excitement I missed him. It took a while to get the 'cast' right a second time, but after about twenty minutes the small iron blue dropped neatly about a foot in front of the fish. There was no drag, it rose, I struck and it was on.   Fortunately it went over the pipe rather than under it and after a good struggle it was netted some thirty metres downstream.

FISH CAUGHT	1 brown trout 4lb	FLY/LURE	Iron Blue - Size 16

Throughout my time in Gloucestershire I fished the little Frome and some other streams when invited, but much of my fishing came on the 'still waters' that were within a days travelling from home. This was fishing, but not the fishing I really wanted. It was not until I returned to Devon that I was able to find fulfilment in untamed waters.

In 1985 I took up a teaching post in Plymouth. Looking for somewhere to live we drew a ten-mile semi circle around the city and sought a family home within easy reach of the new job. The area provided a great deal of choice of locations. There was available city living, moorland villages, coastal towns and rich rural hamlets. Our budget was not unlimited and having to balance the needs of two small children and a wife that did not like to drive we found ourselves in Horrabridge looking at Weir Park House. It met all the family needs and it had fishing at the bottom of the garden. We bought it and moved in during the summer holidays. I hadn't realised it but I had landed in an area steeped in fishing history. Jeffrey (Sou' Wester) Bluett had been a teacher in nearby Tavistock and Major (West Country) Dawson had lived at Brook just fifteen minutes walk away. The local fishing association proved to be the second oldest fishing club in England.

I had to settle in to a new job and this proved a lot more difficult than anticipated. The family also needed settling and the house organising but before long I could explore the generous amount of fishing available.

The river Walkham flowed through the garden and I had riparian rights to 70 yards of river. Above and below were public parks and fishing on these stretches was free to villagers. The river was well stocked with under nourished brown trout but also boasted a decent run of sea trout and a small but unpredictable run of salmon. I had trout and salmon fishing in my garden! Also being just ten miles from Plymouth I had easy access to a great variety of sea fishing. Across the moors there were reservoirs stocked with browns and rainbows. The local fishing association had rights on the four rivers surrounding me and for what, at that time, was a modest sum I was able to buy a permit to the 'ticket waters'.

The move had brought me close to more fishing than I could have hoped for and there was opportunity to regress to childhood and spend every free moment roaming with a rod. Fortunately a combination of work and family curtailed the temptation and prevented me from running in ever decreasing circles trying to wet a line in all the water available.

The association fishing on the rivers, Plym, Meavy, Walkham and Tavy was within easy reach and some within walking distance. I had access to so many miles of water that twenty plus years on there are some sections I have still to fully explore. The stocks of brown trout provided regular sport and the chance of a sea trout or salmon added to the incentive. But the convenient and clear moorland streams rarely gave up their bounty in full daylight and I found it convenient and politic to restrict my fishing to early in the morning (while wife and children slept) or late in evening when all had returned to bed.

I soon become adept at catching brown trout using all manner of wet and dry flies but, although plentiful, Dartmoor trout rarely grow to any great size and do not make good eating. Sea trout were a greater prize but proved to be much more challenging. During the summer months, peal were present in large numbers but catching them proved another thing. I found I could hook one or two by spinning in summer spates and the occasional one came to my trout flies, but it was more by accident than design. I wanted more control. I wanted to be able to catch these bright, silver, hard fighting and superb eating fish on my terms. Gradually

I began to focus my fishing. I couldn't fish everywhere and for every species in the limited leisure time I had, so initially unconsciously, I began to specialise.

I had grown up loving and prizing sea trout and although there was easier fishing to be had, I found I had an opportunity to learn more about the species and how to catch them. Something close to an obsession took over and I worked with determination to discover how to intercept and deceive West Country sea trout.

A couple of nights fishing with the gillie at The Arundel Arms in the late 80s helped a set me up for my quest and allowed me to begin to develop a strategy. I am unhappy in giving endorsements but I should acknowledge the advice I received during those nights. It fast tracked me as a novice sea trout fisheman and provided the platform I needed to gain the knowledge I craved.

These further notes record my obsession and reflect upon my discoveries.

Chapter 2

The Spin

Sea trout returning to fresh water are not active feeders. The prevailing theory being that if the fish returned to the spawning streams with their feeding instincts intact that they would devour and deplete their own offspring. This seems to make some sense but if this is the case then it follows that catching the fish on rod and line is going to present some challenges.

From 1985 I have fished the rivers Tavy, Walkham and Plym almost obsessively. Initially I fished the beats with a spinning rod. With a short rod and a tin of spinners I wandered through the oak woods and over the moors often returning with an empty bag but adding to my of knowledge of the rivers and the fish that inhabit them. Travelling light I could cover a lot of water and my expeditions taught me much about the ways of the sea trout. Although I now much prefer to use a fly rod, working the rivers with spoons and plugs allowed me to get to know the water, find the lies and begin to understand what makes a sea trout take a lure. Looking back this was essential learning. It taught me how to exploit the potential of my fly rod.

When river conditions allowed I would prefer to fish downstream with a Mepps or similar revolving spoon. Following the local practice I worked steadily through the beat making successive down stream casts, allowing the lure to arc round and sweep the river every half metre or so. A size 3 or 4 attracted fish in coloured water and sea trout would rise and hit the lure but often they would avoid getting securely hooked. there were times when I would fail to hook nine out of ten of the fish raised. On these occasions I found that changing to a smaller size spoon could improve results.

But smaller lures had a disadvantage - immature fish invariably found the little lure irresistible and were a constant nuisance.

Spinning with the revolving spoon proved a great attractor and helped me find fish and their lies but I was not catching that many. Sea trout would rise and approach the lure or would 'hit' and then just swim away. The tension on the line would change; I would feel the hit and see a flash of its silver flank. I felt the fish was irritated by the lure and would strike it with its nose but not open its mouth to swallow it. I am sure that many other fish were moved to the spoon but in coloured water they were not seen or felt.

Larger size spinners (Mepps 3 or 4) were often the best attractors. Fish would swirl from the depths (heart stopping stuff), I would see and feel the fish but then it was gone again. When I raised a fish I would cast again over the same spot in the hope that a fish that had 'showed' could be tempted to have another go. But this was inevitably futile. If the fish did come to the lure again it would be with much less enthusiasm. A few times I provoked a fish, or its companion, to rise a second time but it would turn away at a greater distance from the lure and then would not be moved at all. Very rarely I took a fish on a second cast but in hindsight I think this may not have been the one I initially raised, perhaps one that was sharing the lie. Additional casts over the fish would always be ignored and I soon found it was better to move on and find undisturbed lies.

On days when the large spoon raised but failed to hook sea trout I would sometimes change to a smaller lure with better results. But a tiny

DATE	RIVER	BEAT	CONDITIONS
May 1986	Walkham	Magpie	Up and carrying light brown sediment

NOTES

Took off very early and got to the river before it was disturbed and managed to raise a few sea trout. I discovered a new lie at the top of Stinky Pool. Under the alder on the near bank at the neck is a small pot that I had never noticed. I was hit by a large sea trout that was lost after two leaps. It took very close to the bank and I had no time to strike effectively. Next time I must fish this lie from above and may need to stand in the river to cast.

FISH CAUGHT	0	FLY/LURE	Mepps 3 Gold

DATE	RIVER	BEAT	CONDITIONS
July 1986	Walkham	Magpie	Up and carrying light brown sediment

NOTES

The river had risen after overnight rain and was carrying some colour. I elected to fish downstream with a size 3 gold Mepps. Under the Magpie Bridge I raised a fish that hit the spinner but was not hooked. This fish came off the bottom, attacked the spoon and I felt the contact but did not hold the fish. I checked the treble hook. It seemed sharp and functional. I cast repeatedly but the fish would not come again. Ten yards down another sea trout rose and hit the spoon but again remained unhooked. This happened five or six times as I fished down the beat. Sea trout were raised and often nudged the lure but were not hooked.

FISH CAUGHT	0	FLY/LURE	Mepps 3 Gold

DATE	RIVER	BEAT	CONDITIONS
July 1986	Walkham	Magpie	Falling spate

NOTES

I worked down through the Run and Long Pool and raised fish but could not hook them. Fishing likely lies, the spoon attracted fish that would strike and then dive for the bottom. I felt contact with the fish but striking or not striking made no difference.

This was frustrating. Fish were present and were willing to rise but I am not sure they even had their mouths open when they attacked. I changed the lure for a smaller one.

The size 1 Mepps had instant results but not those that I wanted. I immediately started to catch small brown trout that proved difficult to detach from the tiny sharp treble and return unharmed. I avoided the runs and shallows where the small fish would be found and tried the deeper runs and pots. Eventually the next sea trout to rise was not beaten to the spinner by a tiny brown. It was securely hooked and quickly landed.

FISH CAUGHT	Sea trout 1lb 4 oz	FLY/LURE	Mepp 1 Silver

spoon required more accurate casting and a much more careful retrieve. It caught fish but too often the sea trout were beaten to the lure by undersize brown trout or suicidal par. It was something of a blunt instrument that in its crudity produced instant if not gratifying results.

I wanted to get more fish on the bank and so I experimented with a range of lures. I bought all the components and began to make my own spoons, experimenting with blade size, weight and colour. I discovered that large lures were good attractors but smaller lures, if presented carefully could provoke much more positive takes. But there were other factors. The clarity of the water, its speed, depth and the light conditions had roles to play. Conditions ranged as extensively as the contents of my lure box and together they created an infinite number of permutations. I needed to find some patterns and develop some hypotheses to test.

There was clearly a relationship between the lure's size, its distance from the fish and its visibility but it was a complex relationship. I attempted graphs with water clarity, size of lure or distance from the fish on each axis. I am not a scientist or a mathematician but tried to make some calculations and plot points. There were too many variables and I had not the capacity to gather objective data. Much of the action was unseen below the water and when fish and their behaviour could be watched it was fast furious and could not be objectively measured. I could only rely upon my own observations and I could extrapolate, but this was more art than science, but attempting an analytical approach was helpful and did help me formulate something of a hypothesis.

Casting across a stream where I anticipated finding fish and watching sea trout attack the lure has given the impression that the predatory fish operates within two zones. It has a strike zone and surrounding it a window or a visual zone.

Few predators run down their prey over a long distance. Few have the stamina to out run their prey but some can out sprint them. Many predators employ the strategies of waiting in ambush or stealthily stalking prey until it is within striking range. Sea trout, I believe operate similar strategies. They patrol or wait in ambush and when an unsuspecting baitfish comes into range the trap is sprung. The strike range of a sea trout may vary with the size and condition of the fish but does not extend much beyond a metre or two of West Country river.

The fish's visual zone will vary with the available light and the opacity or clarity of the water. When the river is in full spate visibility is probably restricted to a few centimetres. Once it 'fines down', a moorland river may allow a fish to command a visual field of many metres – possibly ten times the strike range. Spinning for sea trout I discovered is at an optimum when the visual zone is a little less than the strike range. On such an occasion the lure will suddenly appear to the fish within its attack zone. At sea the fish must react instantaneously or lose the opportunity and its instinct is triggered. In fresh water it sometimes forgets itself and snaps at such an opportunity. In clearer water the visual zone is extended and if lure is spotted before it enters the strike zone the impulse is tempered. The fish has time to study the lure it may move forward to investigate but it will not be a purposeful attack.

I discovered that there is a positive relationship between the distance a fish was moved to a lure and the chance of it being securely hooked. My observations indicated that when a long distance attack is provoked, by the time the fish has reached the lure it will have changed its mind. Strikes that come from a fish that has moved just a matter of centimetre are more positive and violent than those made by a fish that has travelled to the limits of its strike range. Long-range attacks are often half-hearted affairs and the fish may just 'buzz the lure' and

DATE	RIVER	BEAT	CONDITIONS
June 1998	Plym		

NOTES

Despite some overnight rain the River Walkham had failed to rise or colour up. I drove over to the Plym in the hope that the clay workings may have added some colour but alas it was flowing crystal clear. Despite there being little hope of a fish I set off downstream with a light spinning rod and a size 0 Mepp. This produced nothing of note until I came to the Cliff Pool adjacent to Ham Bushes. Keeping back into the bank so as to remain unseen I cast as far downstream and across as I could. (fine and far off) The small spoon landed on the gravel beside the shrunken stream and as I pulled it into the water it was immediately fishing over a deep gully with a slate overhang. Immediately a fish rose and took the lure. To my surprise a fresh sea trout was soon on the bank.

FISH CAUGHT	1 sea trout 1lb 12oz	FLY/LURE	Mepp 0 Silver

DATE	RIVER	BEAT	CONDITIONS
August 1997	Tavy	Middle	Falling river after spate

NOTES

Having fished down the beat I was returning across the meadow when high above me I could see a lazily flying peregrine. Crossing beneath it and between me and the falcon was a small finch. As I watched the falcon closed its wings and stooped at the unsuspecting bird. It closely passed the finch and swooped up into the air gaining height for another attack. Three times it 'buzzed' the bird before continuing on its journey. Amazingly although it wavered in its flight upon each attack the small bird continued on its course and both departed in different directions.
I believe the peregrine was not at all hungry or perhaps did not have the taste for this particular species but could not resist making a stoop at the small bird in perfect position for an attack.

FISH CAUGHT	1 sea trout 1lb 2oz	FLY/LURE	Size 10 gold special.

DATE	RIVER	BEAT	CONDITIONS
August 1997	Walkham	Magpie	Falling river after spate

NOTES

The river was falling fast and clearing to the colour of pale ale and it was too late to fish downstream. Confident that the water had not been disturbed I fished upstream from Grenofen Bridge with a small Rapala. Casting up and across I systematically targeted chosen lies. There was no response until I arrived at the Viaduct Pool. Here I found a school of peal under the sycamore bush overhanging the far bank. Immediately I cast two fish followed the lure into the shallows before turning away. The next cast resulted in no response. The third cast – a metre upstream resulted in an immediate take. It must have landed in exactly the right place.

FISH CAUGHT	1 sea trout 1lb 8oz	FLY/LURE	Plug CD5 S

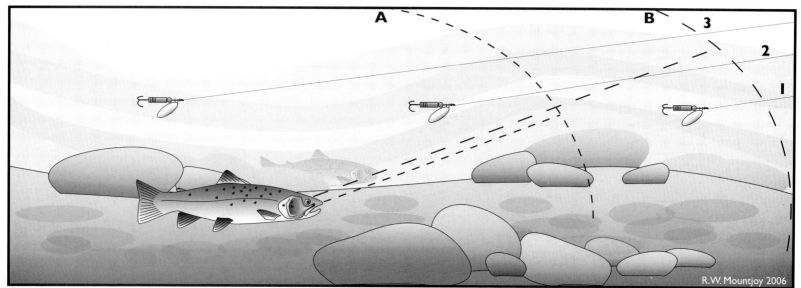

Figure 1.

In the diagram above a sea trout that has taken up a lie in a typical West Country stream. It is summer and the water is low and clear. The arcs, drawn in dotted lines represent the fish's 'strike zone' (labelled A) and its 'visual zone' (labelled B). These are not drawn to any scale but to represent the difference in size of the two distances in these conditions.

A fisherman works downstream fishing a rotating spoon. On the first cast the lure is seen as soon as it reaches the fish's visual zone (B). The fish sees the lure but it is outside its strike zone and it has time to check its predatory instincts. It may rise but will abort any attack. Cast 2 passes through the strike zone but the lure has already been seen and rejected by the fish and it will be ignored. Cast 3 falls behind the fish and is not seen.

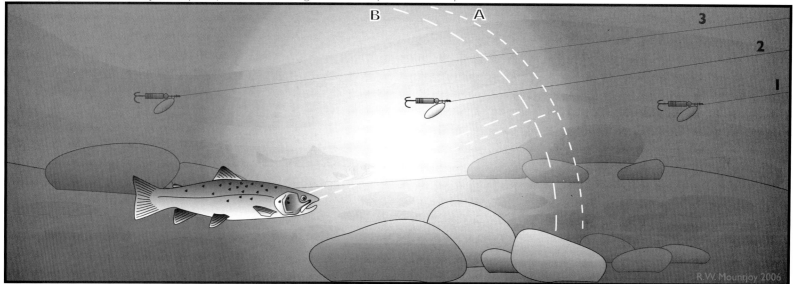

Figure 2

The river has risen and coloured after heavy rain. The fish's visual zone has reduced (arc B). It is now just within the fish's strike zone (arc A) and any lure that is seen may be attacked. Cast 1 has passed outside of this zone will not be seen and will not raise or disturb the fish. This is the optimum time to spin for sea trout.

DATE	RIVER	BEAT	CONDITIONS
July 1991	River Walkham		Clearing but still high

NOTES

The river had cleared but had yet to drop to summer levels. I worked up stream from Grenofen Bridge with a light spinning rod and a small plug. The 'Chip Shop' pool looked promising and I stepped down the bank to keep my silhouette as low as possible and cast from the best vantage point. The first cast over the sill resulted in an immediate take. I struck and without delay managed to pull the small peal over the edge and back into the fast water towards me. This ensured it did not disturb any remaining fish but meant it took some controlling. But before long it came to the net and was in the bag. Returning to my position another identical cast resulted in another take. The same trick was tried and a fish took but it was a little larger and was lost in the fast water. A third cast in the same place provoked no response and so I cast again but a metre upstream. No response. I cast again another metre upstream and instantly got a powerful take. This time I allowed the fish to run. I think I had no choice. The fish ran to the head of the pool and leapt – summer salmon! After its leap the fish decided to sulk and although I it took some time it too was netted and bagged.

FISH CAUGHT	1 sea trout 14 oz 1 salmon 5lb 4 oz	FLY/LURE	CD5 S

DATE	RIVER	BEAT	CONDITIONS
August 1997	Plym	Shaugh	Falling river after spate

NOTES

The river was clearing fast and was too clear for downstream spinning in most runs and pools. A few casts down favourite runs confirmed this but I had no fly rod with me. I decided to target those lies where I could approach and cast from unseen stands. A stiff walk took me to the cauldron where in these conditions I had possibly two casts before any fish would be spooked. From behind the holly trees I flicked a small spinner out across the boulders on the near side. It landed short and the retrieve produced nothing. A second cast is the right spot was futile but I did it anyway. The remaining lie up near the streamy water would have been undisturbed and so I adjusted my position and cast up towards the head. This time the line ran sweetly and the small Mepp hit the right spot. Immediately it was hit by a small peal that was landed in the tail.

FISH CAUGHT	1 sea trout 14oz	FLY/LURE	Mepp 1

DATE	RIVER	BEAT	CONDITIONS
August 2004	Tavy	Abbey	Low and clear

NOTES

The river had returned to summer levels and almost all colour from the previous day's rain had been washed away. I had intended to use a light spinning rod but this was unlikely to provide any sport in these conditions. Fortunately I also had a fly rod in the car and this was set up with more hope than faith. Working upstream I found a shoal of peal in the Abbey Pool. I cast as gently as I could up beyond and in front of the shoal. I let the fly sink and then allowed it to drift back across the bottom to lift it just in front of the school. I had probably just the one chance. To my delight a small fish turned and took the fly. Before long I had an 8 oz 'schoolie' on the bank.

FISH CAUGHT	1 sea trout 8oz	FLY/LURE	Weighted GRHE Size 12.

turn away or may hit it with its mouth closed and then return to its lie. There may be no intention to kill or eat it but just an inability to resist having a swipe at it. I have seen birds of prey do similar things when they have not been hungry but have been irritated by small birds that have blundered into tempting range.

Initially I thought that the added time the sea trout had to travel to the lure enabled a more careful examination and this is what reduced the chances of a take. I thought that aborted attacks were down to a realisation that the lure was a deception. If this was the case I deduced that more realistic lures may lead to greater success. I experimented extensively with minnows and small, very realistic plugs. The more naturally coloured plugs, I found often have the edge. They result in more positive takes in clearer water but any advantage is possibly outweighed by the relative expense. The expensive plug does impede risky casting and there are times when accurate casting is a more important factor.

I suggest that the sea trout is not thinking about the item it is attacking. It is responding to an instinct. – a prey that suddenly appears in the strike zone is attacked – there is not time to inspect it and check if it is edible or weigh up the pros and cons of attacking it. When at sea and feeding, if the sea trout delayed an attack to examine the prey it would swim away and a meal lost. The lure must trigger the attack instinct and quite crude devices can do this. More realistic lures have the advantage that they, like the prey they imitate, are not so visible and so are less likely to be seen until they are within the fish's strike zone. This makes the naturalistic plug the weapon of choice as the river clears.

As I began to learn the lies on my rivers I began to target them with carefully aimed casts. Calculating where the fish would be most likely to be lying, I would try to drop the lure into the fish's strike zone and begin the retrieve

immediately. This has called for careful and accurate casting and at times a half-mile walk for just a couple of casts. But these casts if delivered effectively could result in two fish in the bag and all I could want from a morning's fishing.

When heavy rain has coloured the river and the water has lost its usual clarity I try to cover the known lies methodically. I cast so that the lure is swept through the taking zones as it travels across the stream in the traditional 'down and across' approach. Starting above the lies work towards them with successive casts moving across the river in concentric arcs. With a lure of the right size for the conditions this produces consistent results. See Fig. 4

In clearing water I avoid fishing the water down to a lie in successive sweeps and do not I stand in one place and fan out casts around me as I would with a fly at night. Even more pointless is wandering up and down casting here and there without any strategy. It is important to approach each lie from a position outside the window of any fish and make a plan. I commend novices to stop at every pool and think about how they are going to fish it before they begin. Work out where fish are likely to be lying and how one can cover them without disturbing others.

Usually I work my way upstream to remain unseen by fish that will be facing into the current. If I wade, more often than not, the shoals of small frightened trout run upstream and spook the larger sea trout. It is better to crawl up the bank to a position where the lie can be reached and advantage can be taken of the cover available. It is important that the sea trout does not see the fisherman or the lure before the latter is within striking range. This may require a few practice casts from one stand before changing position to cover the intended lies. I try to work out the best order to fish the over the potential takers and how to avoid spooking fish that are placed lower down the list.

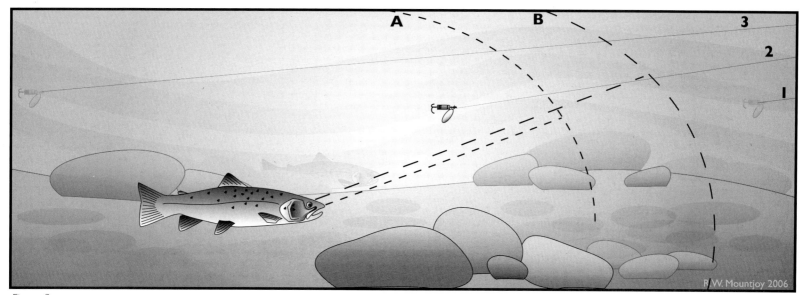

Figure 3

The river has begun to fall and clear and the fish's visual zone has increased to B. It is close, but beyond the strike zone. Fewer, widely spread, more careful and selective casts are required. Repeated casting over hot spots will not be rewarded. Clumsy casts will disturb fish and a smaller more realistic lure is more likely to bring results. As it becomes clearer fishing upstream will be more productive.

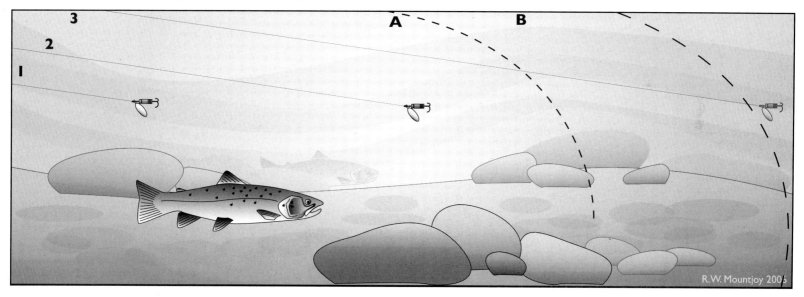

Figure 4

The river has almost returned to summer levels and clarity. The fish will see a downstream worked lure before it reaches its strike zone (and may also see a fisherman moving towards it). It is time to start fishing upstream with small lures. Cast 1 falls behind the fish and if not too close will not disturb it. Cast 2 lands within the strike zone and if it immediately begins to spin it is likely to raise the fish. Cast 3 is too far in front of the fish and will be ignored even as it passes over the fish.

I may make some casts in the tail and some in the head before returning to the tail to cover the middle of the pool. Each and every pool is different and this changes once again with the river levels. It is impossible to be prescriptive as every pool and every day will require a revision of tactics. It is worth a few minutes to stand back from each pool or run and think through the best approach.

Fishing upstream I have been able to surprise a fish by flicking a lure in front of it and bringing it back before they have had chance to realise what has really entered their space. A cast too far ahead of the fish will give too much time to see the lure coming. It is often tempting to cast up beyond the lie bring the lure back past the fish. Although this often produces fish at dusk, in daylight it is certain to spook every fish in the pool. It is far better to work up through the pool with successive carefully targeted casts as shown in Fig1.

Occasionally an obstacle will conveniently restrict the fish's window and this can allow a fish to be surprised with a carefully placed lure. Lies on tight bends in the stream, against a ledge or between boulders can sometimes allow a lure to be swung across a fish and shock it into taking. Even in clear water. Those deep little pockets of water between boulders in a run or beneath an undercut bank can sometimes produce a fish in less than ideal conditions. Using broken water as cover a fisherman who can keep below the sky line can often reach 'un-spooked' fish and provoke it with an unexpected offer.

Once I discovered that it was possible to take fish in this way I began to seek out lies where the same trick would work and have found new and sometimes unusual places to take fish. The problem with the method is that you only get one chance and its success depends on finding undisturbed fish that you can catch unawares. If you make a bad cast and have to try again it is unlikely to work - as there is now no surprise.

My experiences have helped me form the theory that a sea trout is driven by two conflicting instincts when it returns to fresh water. It has been a predator foremost but now it is also a potential parent. Its predatory instincts are suppressed by its reproductive drives but aggressive feeding impulses may be set off if the fish is caught unawares. When able to watch a lure coming towards its strike zone the fish's predatory impulses can be controlled and while it may move to investigate it is unlikely to attack with any real intent. If caught by surprise and given insufficient time to allow its parental conditioning to come into play the fish will often attack, This does not happen on every occasion but with sufficient frequency to guide the tactics of the sea trout enthusiast.

The key element of successful sea trout fishing is a matter of presenting a lure of appropriate size, within the fish's striking range and with sudden and complete surprise. Once a fish has seen the lure and decided to ignore the offering or abort an attack it will not be induced to rise again. It seems that a fish that has made the rash gesture of attacking the lure and missed, aborted the strike or took half heartedly, immediately exhausts its predatory energy. Fish do have memories and reasearch at Plymouth University has confirmed that rainbow trout can remember stimulii for three months or more. Sea trout are unlikely to be tricked a second time. This has become the principle upon which I have subsequently based all of my sea trout fishing and is a theme I will be retuning to throughout these notes.

Travelling light, with a spinning rod enabled me to cover a lot of water and tease a great many fish. It taught me a lot but I finally came to realise that the spinning rod has its limitations. I often found myself frustrated by my inability to offer a small lure with the finesse I really needed.

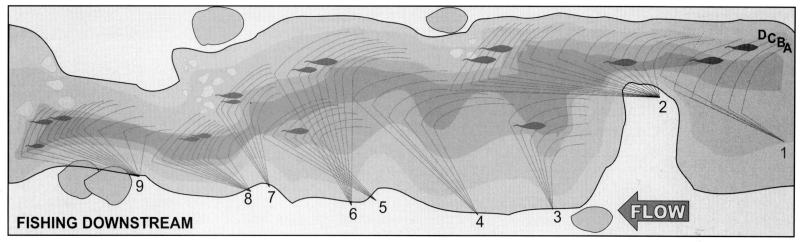

Fig 5

The river is in spate and carrying colour and sediment. Fish have spread out and have taken up lies on the edge of the main flows. The river is fished downstream - sweeping the river with successive casts that swing across the current and the lies. All taking water is covered and the 'hot spots' may be given more attention with more closely grouped casts. But repetitive casting over one place is unproductive and should be avoided. As the river drops the casts are fewer and more distanced until it is too clear to make downstream casting effective.

Tha angler begins at stand 1. at the head of the pool and casts to A allowing the lure to swing with the current before retrieving. He or she then makes successive downstream casts (B,C and then D) until the next group of lies may be better covered from another position (2).

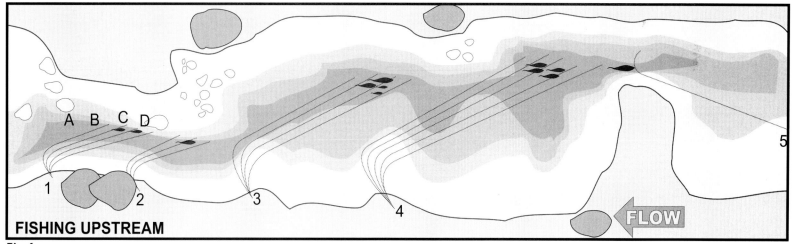

Fig 6

The river has dropped to typical summer levels and is running clear and fish have moved into the deeper channels.

Fishing downstream would be unproductive and would just spook sea trout. Selective casts are made working upstream. Fewer casts are necessary and these must be more accurately placed. A smaller and more naturalistic lure is used (a fly would be better). It is important that the first time the sea trout sees the lure it is within its strike zone. Starting at stand 1 a cast to A is made and brought back faster than the current. The next cast is made about two metres upstream to B and retrieved in the same way. Then C and D. Once these lies have been covered with a few well targeted casts the angler then moves to stand 2 and covers the next piece of water in the same way . It is important to cast from positions where the fish (facing upstream) will not see the approaching angler.

Having arrived at the head of this particular pool, a long downstream cast may be made to cover any fish in the neck (more likely to be a summer salmon). This cannot be covered from downstream but an outcrop of rock provides some convenient cover and salmon are less fussy.

There are times when I wanted to drift the lure to to a place where I could then pull it across an unsuspecting fish. I wanted to allow it to be be carried by the current, bouncing amongst the pebbles and stones and be invisible until it was right on the fish's nose. Then, if lifted away it could induce the take I hoped for.

I felt I wanted a lure that could enter the water silently and make less noise travelling through the stream. Inevitably I turned once more to the fly rod. There was nothing philosphical or sociological in this decision. It was not driven by any prejudice, I just thought that the fly could catch more fish in a greater range of conditions.

After heavy rain when the river is dark and coloured, if I want to grab a hour or so of fishing I am as likel;y as not pick up a spinning rod. Not because it is better tool for the job - even in heavy water. It is just an easier one to use. Also a spinning rod allows you to cover more river in the time available. In some ways it is a bit like fast food - immediately rewarding but ultimately less satisfying.

Chapter 3

The Lie

My first year's fishing the Tavy, Walkham and Plym with a spinning rod served as an apprenticeship of sorts and taught me something about sea trout and their behaviour. Advised by those older and wiser, I swept the beats with successive casts and discovered every, snag, pot, gully and ledge. I found out where sea trout are most likely to be found and where they may be tempted to rise and take a lure. Eventually I discovered where to find brown trout, where to find sea trout and where to find salmon and by selective casting I could sometimes find and target species.

It is often said that 90% of fish will be found in 10% of the water and my experience has proved that there are large sections of my home rivers which despite seeming as inviting and beautiful as all the rest, fail to produce a single fish. Fish obviously pass through these barren areas but if they do stay they find my lures resistible. There are runs and pools that I have regularly fished in all manner of ways that invariably fail to produce even a hungry brownie while there are others where I know there will be fish, which if have been undisturbed, will rise to my fly.

Finding the hot spots has been a matter of experience, combined with the knowledge generously passed on by the old-timers supplemented by some acumen. I have combed my home stretches with flies and lures and noted where fish have been raised, where fish have been taken and recorded the information in my diary. Analysing the known lies and looking for similar conditions elsewhere on the river I have been able to discover more taking places to add to my list. This has helped me to decide where to focus attention and where time is best spent when it is in short supply.

When I have the luxury of a whole day to fish I will work my way through the whole beat systematically. I will explore the considered unproductive stretches and try to find new lies while, practising my casting and enjoying the environment. On such days I might keep the known hot spots, like the choicest deserts until last. When pressed for time or suffering from withdrawal symptoms – I confess I sometimes rush to the river hit a few favourite taking places and drag myself away to other duties.

While I have much appreciated the advice given to me by my generous old-timers I have found it equally rewarding to find my own hot spots. Alas, not everyone has twenty seasons or so to spend finding the good taking places or the time to cultivate old-timers so that they will divulge their secrets. I hope that my notes may help those who, new to a river or a beat and wanting or needing to find fish, to work out where fish may lie and where the occasional sea trout may be taken.

Sea trout returning to a river need to find a place of safety to stay until spawning time arrives and they move to the gravel beds. Spawning takes place in relatively shallow water where fast flows sort the stones into conveniently sized deposits. These places provide little cover and the fresh sea trout in its silver, blue and lilac livery does not have the best camouflage for the gold and reds of the shallow riffles. Until it has changed into its spawning colours the fish needs cover, shade and space to run if threatened.

DATE	RIVER	BEAT	CONDITIONS
July 1989 Day	Plym		Clearing river after overnight rain. Peat stain

We had heavy rain last night and the Walkham was a roaring torrent with much debris being carried. I turned my attention to the Plym and found this river to be high and darkly coloured but carrying much less debris. Fishing down from Shaugh Bridge I found no fish in any of the pools but was surprised to get a take at my feet in less than ten centimetres of water. I carried on fishing the margins with greater care and took a brace of peal. Both fish were taken within centimetres from the bank in water no more than ankle deep.

FISH CAUGHT	2 sea trout 1lb 2 oz and 1 lb 4 oz	FLY/LURE	Bluebottle Fly. Treble 12.

DATE	RIVER	BEAT	CONDITIONS
June 1986 Day	Walkham	Magpie	Heavy spate – much debris

NOTES
A very heavy river with much debris and I was about to give up when I met one of the old boys. I was bemoaning the conditions and the lack of sport when he opened his bag to show me two fine peal. "How, where, when?" were my questions! "I'll show you lad (I was 43 at the time)" he replied and took me to a deep run where subsidence had scooped a small bay from the bank. Here he dibbled his fly in the slack water and as he retrieved a sea trout rose but turned back before hitting the lure. "That's the way," he pronounced and shuffled off leaving me to try. The fish, if they remained had been teased too many times and my efforts were unrewarded. (In subsequent spates I was able to copy the trick with success!)

FISH CAUGHT	0	FLY/LURE	1" tube

DATE	RIVER	BEAT	CONDITIONS
June 1995 Day	Plym.	Shaugh	Clearing

NOTES
A falling river after heavy overnight rain. Opaque and swift with colour coming from a combination of peat and china clay waste. Two fish came to a weighted treble fished across the run from Mac's Pool. Both taken from a channel between the boulders a third lost. Fished down to the bridge by which time the river had fallen and was running clear. Returned to Mac's pool and found the school had moved further up into the holes near the head. Took one on an upstream weighted fly and lost another.

FISH CAUGHT	3 sea trout 3lb, 1 ½ lb, 2 ¼ lb	FLY/LURE	Bluebottle Fly Treble 12/ Leaded GRHE Size 14

The returning fish, having fought their way up from the sea are careful to conserve energy. For the most part they will not eat and have to survive possibly seven months or more before they can run once more to sea. They are adjusting to changes in the salinity of the water, their body fat is being used up and they are preparing for the only sex they may ever have. They have to behave sensibly to survive but are edgy and nervous. While some occasionally thrash about and leap, for most of the time they lie still and quiet, taking up lies that allow them to expend minimal energy. They become 'lazy fish' and to a noticeable degree they will favour quieter pockets of our racing streams.

When the river is in spate quieter pockets are in short supply but the sea trout are masters at using the eddies and diverted flows from obstacles in the path of the river to find cosy spots where the demands on their energy are limited. These change and move when the flow recedes and so does the sea trout to find another comfortable spot. Sea trout lies must therefore move when the height of the river changes - see chapter 2 Figs. 5 and 6.

As the river rises the force of water through the main pool will sap energy and the fish will move out to the fringes or drop to the micro conditions between the rocks and pebbles. They seem to enjoy the pebbly runs beyond the tails of pools where the many obstacles must create little pockets of comfort and security. A heavy fly that will pierce the fast flow but float across the current and over these lies can incite aggressive takes and often from the better fish.

When the river is high and running fast it is difficult to understand how anything can survive on the bed of a spate river. With all manner of debris being carried by the flood and silt, sand, gravel and even large stones moving along the bottom. It is no surprise that sea trout find their preferred places uncomfortable and they seek out shelter in the margins of the stream.

Fishing in such conditions is challenging as a long line is inevitably hung with grass, leaves, twigs and other debris before the lure on the end gets near a fish. In such conditions I prefer to leave the river and return when it is beginning to 'fine down' but this is not always possible and I learnt form one of my old-timers that when everything seems against it you can still take fish. He showed me small bays in the banks that were not large enough to suck in eddies but were large enough to create havens of gentle flow. In normal conditions they were places where fish would be vulnerable and would be avoided and he called them 'spate lies' Here he demonstrated how he could take fish by flicking a lure into the edge of flow, allowing it to sweep into the slack water and retrieve immediately. In dark water he would cover a bay of about a metre in length and half in depth with about ten successive casts. It took some practice but I have been able to emulate him and fish have appeared under the edge to lunge at a fly almost at my feet

During summer levels sea trout are to be found near deep water but not necessarily in it. The depths of a large pool provide security but the pressure at the bottom may be a little uncomfortable. When they feel safe sea trout will drift back to the pool tail and shallow fringes, the quiet corners and the gentle back eddies. There may exist an optimum depth where the water pressure creates the right degree of comfort but a large pool can provide the safety of deep water but also shallows where the fish will prefer to rest when all is quiet. Although fish will be found in the shallow runs and riffles more will be found within a short dash of a deep hole.

When undisturbed and at rest sea trout prefer a gentle flow and will be happy hugging the clean gravel bottom of relatively shallow water. Preferring depths of less than a metre they will be found close to obstructions that slow and redirect the power of a stream and provide

DATE	RIVER	BEAT	CONDITIONS
July 1999 Day	Walkham	Walkham Lower	Low and clear

NOTES

The river was low and clear and although the chances of a fish werenon existent I took up the rod and walked the Magpie Beat. At Grenofen I stood on the bridge and watched the shoals of sea trout gathering in Mr Pawson's Pool. Larger fish (and some salmon) were lying in the depths below the bridge while the smaller peal had fanned out across the tail of the pool in water of 10 – 30 centimetres. Morning sunshine was breaking through the trees and the smaller fish seemed to be concentrated in the sunlit sections. A bird flew over and its shadow caused the fish to scatter. I remained motionless and watched. Gradually they drifted back to the shallows at the tail but this time they avoided the sunshine

FISH CAUGHT		FLY/LURE	

DATE	RIVER	BEAT	CONDITIONS
June 1999 Day	Walkham		

NOTES

The river was low and clear but carrying a trace of colour. I found a small shoal of sea trout in the Viaduct Pool and approached from down stream. Sunshine was coming over my right shoulder and the shadows of the fish gave away their presence before I saw the fish themselves. I cast with the greatest delicacy I could master just beyond the group and retrieved delicately. The fly dropped perfectly and with no splash from the line but the fish immediately scattered.

FISH CAUGHT		FLY/LURE	

DATE	RIVER	BEAT	
July 2001 Day	Plym.	Shaugh	Clearing

NOTES

The river was falling and clearing and so I took a fly rod and worked my way upstream with a weighted fly. I had no luck until I came to Ham Fields where there are three successive pools with rapid flows in between. The top pool has a frequently inhabited lie near the tail against the left bank. A weighted Blue Bottle was dropped into the haven of tranquillity that was encircled with turmoil and immediately taken by a powerful fish. It took off downstream between the boulders forcing me into the stream to follow. Fortunately the tiny treble had a good hold and the fish was eventually landed.

FISH CAUGHT	1 sea trout 3lb	FLY/LURE	Bluebottle treble 14

Fig 1

In heavy water sea trout find shelter in the margins and amongst the stones and boulders.
The deep channels will be scoured by strong currents carrying debris. Loitering here will be hard work but mongst the pebbles in shallow water or hard against the bank there is refuge.

Fig 2.

Undisturbed sea trout have drifted back to the tail of the pool where they enjoy gentle flows in very shallow water. In clear water it is very difficult to take fish from such positions. They are easily spooked and a shadow will send the fish sliding into the depths. After dark it is another matter - these become the places to find taking fish.

DATE	RIVER	BEAT	CONDITIONS
June 1988 Day	Plym	Shaugh	Low clear

NOTES

The river was very low and clear but holding good stocks of sizeable sea trout. Unfortunately the river is being constantly disturbed by groups camping in the valley and enjoying the exceptionally hot weather. A swing has been set up over the Scout Hut Pool and the campers are plunging into one of the best holding pools from it. I have found a group bathing in the river using copious amounts of shampoo! The fish seem to have left those pools altogether and I left the river without fishing

Two days later I found the beat full of dead fish. Walking the top half to Shaugh Bridge I counted 30 sea trout lying on the bottom – all in the 2 – 5lb class – heartbreaking! I retrieved an example and took to the local river warden who diagnosed furunculosis. I have often wondered if the detergent had had a detrimental effect on the fish's protective slime.

FISH CAUGHT	0	FLY/LURE	

DATE	RIVER	BEAT	CONDITIONS
September 1999 Day	Tavy	Upper	High and clear

NOTES

The river remained above normal summer levels but was running clear. I was fishing for salmon with a fly rod and a small tube fly. Having reached the end of the beat with no success I set about fishing the last pool with little optimism The head of the pool was narrow with a small waterfall of about one metre. I thought that it would provide my last chance of the day. I made a short cast and drew the fly back through the stream of bubbles. As I was about to lift to cast again to my astonishment a large sea trout rose through the white water and took the fly like a brownie. After much leaping and thrashing the fish was drawn to the tail where it was netted. It was a dark heavily spotted fish of about 3lb and it was returned to the water. I returned to the head of the pool and the next cast produced an identical rise and take. This time it was a salmon that dived for the bottom and sulked with a shaking head under the broken stream. Eventually it was coaxed out and after a few short runs it too was netted at the tail.

FISH CAUGHT	1 sea trout about 3lb returned. 1 salmon	FLY/LURE	Blue and pearl copper tube ½"

DATE	RIVER	BEAT	CONDITIONS
April 2000 Day	Plym	Shaugh	Low – a little silt being carried

NOTES

The river was clearing after some rain and I probably arrived too late to have any real chance of success and I had brought a spinning rod and box of Mepps. In Ham Pool I found a large sea trout lying 'in station' in the middle of the stream and between beds of slate. My over optimistic offer of a size 2 Mepp was ignored but the fish was not worried. It remained in its lie but occasionally moved from side to side. I crept closer and watched. The fish was taking tadpoles that had washed out of riverside pools and were drifting downstream. What I would have given for a fly rod and a small black fly!

FISH CAUGHT	0	FLY/LURE	

some cover. They like the hiding places provided by overhanging banks, roots and rock sills but especially runs filled with boulders and large pebbles. There are inevitably micro conditions in the flows between large stones and sea trout clearly find such places favourable. A good long pebbly run with pots of metre or so deep will often provide homes for small groups of sea trout. By changing position marginally the fish can accommodate changes in the pace and depth of the stream and such runs provide good taking places in all conditions.

A favoured pool on the Plym has deep holes at the head where fish can seek security if disturbed but a long run filled with pebbles and boulders at its tail. The tail is overhung with alder and hazel and provides the perfect resting place for returning sea trout. In low water there is always a fish in the head of the pool that will respond to an upstream weighted fly. When darkness comes these fish will ease back to spend the night amongst the water worn stones in the shallow tail. From here they will slash at wake flies fished over and between the boulders. In heavy water the tail will be filled with fish that will lunge at lures swung across the stream.

A creature with no eyelids probably finds bright sunshine tiresome and although at times sea trout seem to be basking in the sunshine at the tail of pools they are more likely to be found in shaded lies. On some large pools they will move around with the sun and lie in the shadows formed. In sunshine fish are also more visible to terrestrials and as such subject themselves to greater danger. Often we see the shadow of the fish on the riverbed before we see the fish but shadows can provide early warning and on seeing them fish will dash for safety.

Sunlight must provide confusing shadows and reflections and hinder a fish's ability to use its excellent eyesight to full advantage. Fish in sunny lies are easily spooked and are not, in my

experience good takers. Any shadow crossing their line of vision sends the fins quivering and any further movement drives them to the depths or under rocks and stones.

Sea trout are known to like well-oxygenated water but fighting the fast turbulent flows that invigorate the stream for any length of time would exhaust their energy. The fish can often be found around the edges of broken water. Here they can take advantage of the oxygen rich waters without having to battle with it. A lure that appears out of a gush of white water and across the nose of a sea trout can provoke an impulsive take. Sea trout will be regularly found in small holes amidst fast and furious flows. These are difficult fish to engage mainly because the small slot gives insufficient space for the fish to see the lure and turn to take it. They are best approached from above when the water is coloured but on small clear streams you sometimes have no choice but to cast to them from below.

The rivers Plym and Walkham both have sections where the river runs down a staircase of small pools and falls. From the appearance of the first bluebells to the fall of the first sycamore leaf each of these will become home to a sea trout or two. When all is quiet they will drift back with their tails practically on the sill of the pool, when troubled they can ease forward and hide under the ledges. These are difficult lies to cover as there is limited room for a fly to swing and the fish to rise.

An upstream cast with a weighted fly thrown into the fall and then allowed to tumble with it before being brought back faster than the current can take an occasional fish. Fish lying alongside the stream of bubbles from the fall seem to be unable to resist something that appears suddenly out of the cascade. In coloured water a goldhead can be fished from above using a sink and draws action as it is swept to the tail. There is a risk of taking

DATE	RIVER	BEAT	CONDITIONS
August 1992 Day	Plym	Shaugh	River up and carrying some sediment and colour

NOTES

I fished the Shaugh to Bickleigh section of the Plym this morning and took two 'schoolies' from the tail of Scout Hut Pool on a small Blue Bottle. It was a pleasant day – no one else was fishing and so I continued downstream. Between the boulders at the tail of the Cauldron I had a savage take from a large sea trout. This fish fought like a demon but was eventually netted in Ham Pool a couple of hundred yards below. It weighed 4lb 5 oz but upon cleaning was found to contain a small brown trout of about four inches and a smaller salmon parr. I think this is the only time I have found browns or parr in the stomach of a sea trout.

FISH CAUGHT	3 sea trout 12 oz, 12 oz and 4lb 5oz.	FLY/LURE	Bluebottle Size 12 Treble

DATE	RIVER	BEAT	CONDITIONS
August 2003 Day	Tavy	Abbey	Low and clear. Bright breezy afternoon 18 C

NOTES

The river was low and clear but there was a good upstream breeze and so I was fishing upstream with a fly rod and weighted nymph. In the run above the Abbey Pool I took two sea trout. One came from midstream but the larger and heavily spotted fish was taken from close to the near bank and below a spreading oak tree. This fish of 1lb 8 oz was full of large green caterpillars. It hit the fly as soon as it plopped into the water - I am not sure that its similarity with the insects in its gut was a factor - I think this is the first time I have taken a sea trout that has been feeding on such items.

FISH CAUGHT	2 sea trout 1lb and 1lb 8 oz	FLY/LURE	Czech Nymph Yellow/Black Size 14

DATE	RIVER	BEAT	CONDITIONS
July 2004 night	Tavy	Middle	Low clear overcast 13 C

NOTES

Took one fish from the tail of the big pool and continued down to the run out with confidence. Allowed the flies to drift around the big boulder at the tail where a fish had been showing. Got caught up and lost my flies but tackled up once again and continued – just when I thought I should retrieve or I would become snagged again I had a savage take and after a good battle had a fine fish in the net.

FISH CAUGHT	2 sea trout 3lb and 1 lb.	FLY/LURE	Special size 10.

Fig 3

In low and high water sea trout seek out the shelter and security offered by the micro conditions found in pebble filled runs. These are often good places to find taking fish.

Fig 4

The flow of bubbles created when water cascades over a ledge creates good cover and near the bottom the flow is gentle but well oxygenated. Sea trout will stack up in such places - especially in hot weather but it is difficult to present them with an enticing lure.

unwanted browns using this tactic and it has caught some of the very shy heavyweights.

In warm weather sea trout may be forced to seek out the vigorous flows as the quieter sections of the river become 'stale'. Fish in need of oxygen sometimes prefer the swift broken streams at the head of pools or the fast turbulent runs between them. At times they will be found where salmon like to lie under the stream of bubbles flowing from water tumbling into the pools. These can be taken by a lure cast up into the cascade to be pulled by the water down into the cauldron and then retrieved just before it hits the bottom.

In the hottest of weather many fish will be in need of oxygen and they will populate the runs and necks of pools. These are usually fish that have been stressed by high temperature or disturbance. These rarely make good 'takers' of any lure. Stressed fish use up excess energy and become susceptible to disease. Fish are conditioned to cope with sudden

shocks and disturbances and will be used to animals entering the water to cool or drink and birds flying over and landing in the water. Normal fishing activity probably causes less stress to fish than these natural events such as duck landing in the water but during periods of drought these fish are probably best left undisturbed during daytime. Our attentions can create unacceptable stress and when rivers are low in oxygen it can lead to fatalities.

Fresh run fish also enjoy fast runs and many will be found on the edge of white water at the heads of pools. These may be enjoying the well-oxygenated water or resting before making another dash through the rapids. These are difficult lies to fish but are worth the effort. If there is sufficient cover, a lure allowed to drift down the stream fluttering in and out of the fast water can work. A 'dibbled' lure can sometimes produce savage takes but as the season progresses these places are more likely to be taken up by salmon that will take a lure with more audacity.

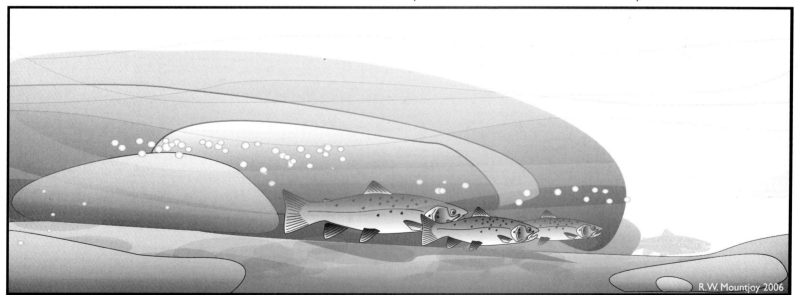

Fig 5
In low water or when disturbed sea trout will pack themselves into the spaces between overhanging boulders or against rock ledges. They may take up residence and wait until it is time to move out and onto the spawning gravels.

Sone sea trout find it difficult to cast off their predatory instincts and may take up lies where they would expect to intercept prey. Although these fish are rarely actively feeding, they are clearly drawn to such places. Perhaps the position just feels right! If other factors (shade, security, energy conservation, etc.) are not playing a part they will happily take up a feeding station like brown trout.

In places where you would expect to find taking brown trout, peal may be found throughout the summer. Frequently they favour gaps between boulders and large stones, places that would provide a steady stream of food items to feeding fish but also provide some shelter from the full flow. Fish in feeding lies may be takers in all conditions as the predatory instinct may already have been partly triggered but there is an increased chance of being beaten to the lure by a hungry brown.

If you can place yourself in position to watch a large shoal of sea trout in an undisturbed pool you will see some from time to time, take up a station in the flow and near the surface in readiness to take drifting prey. Occasionally they will rise and seem to inspect something floating overhead and frequently appear to take something from the surface. These will always be small school peal and are often immature fish that may not spawn on this return. I have tried to tempt such fish with a dry fly but with limited success. There are records of good catches elsewhere but, try as I will, I have yet to enjoy such rewards. I have taken them when casting for browns and a sea trout has taken me by surprise but this is exceptional.

Individual sea trout do give in to their feeding instincts and occasionally some do begin to feed again once in the rivers. Possibly most sea trout take some items of potential food but few actually swallow them. It is not common but every year I catch a few fish that have been actively feeding. I now give the intestines of any

sea trout taken a cursory glance when cleaning and unless I see something obvious I do not carry out a close inspection but for many years I examined the gut of every fish caught with some thoroughness (564 fish over 12 years) and recorded any contents.

Fish caught on the river Plym in spate conditions, sometimes contained slugs. I have never found this documented elsewhere but in certain sections of the river during summer spates one in ten fish had eaten slugs and some were gorged with them. The slugs were small olive molluscs about the size of a baked bean or slightly larger. The fish that had taken them were usually larger fish in excess of 2lb and heavily spotted. They were obviously not fresh run fish and had probably been in the river three or more months. They came to the rod in the later part of the season and were caught from lies adjacent to small tributaries or streams that ran off the moor.

A few fish (about 10% on the Plym) caught in spates had taken small olive nymphs. These were usually smaller and fresher fish and were taken from the runs between pools in classic feeding lies. Looking retrospectively through my diaries these may well have been immature fish on their first return to the river and not destined to spawn on this visit. On a few occasions I caught larger sea trout in similar locations that had taken other fish and a couple of times I caught fresh run fish with shrimps and sand eels amongst the stomach contents. Never have I caught a fish with a worm in its gut.

None of the fish I have taken from the river Walkham have contained significant food items but downstream on the Tavy, I have sometimes caught sea trout that have recently dined. The food items have included caterpillars, nymphs, beetles or small black flies but never very many and most fish (98%) have completely empty guts. These fish have also been mature fish that have resided in the river for some

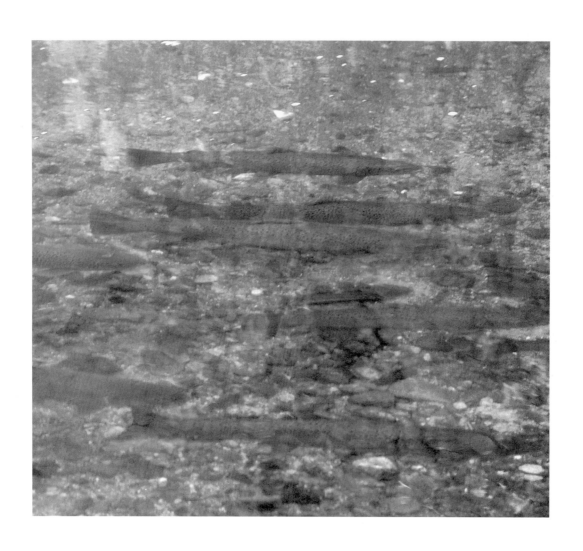

months. Usually the feeders are caught late in the season and come from lies where you might expect to take feeding brown trout. The flesh of such fish is often of inferior quality and I now return late season fish that have a dark or stale appearance. Many of these may have also been feeding but the small bright Tavy 'harvest peal' make excellent eating and are more often bagged. always have empty guts.

'Feeding lies' are worth seeking out and fishing with fresh sea trout in mind but may not produce fresh fish. While I still fish these places I have tended to look elsewhere for the majority of my catch. I now tend to take most of my sea trout from the larger pools where there are shallow fringes and shade is cast from overhanging trees. I am lucky to have access to pools where fish can rest and wait for autumn in comfort and security. Fish of all sizes can congregate in these special places for when danger threatens they can dive to the depths and pack themselves under ledges and rocks. At night they will drift back to the tails or move up to the well-oxygenated runs. After dark these are the places I most enjoy fishing the fly.

There is nothing more enjoyable on a warm night than lazily throwing out a tiny fly and then fishing it as slow as you dare across those little gullies at the neck or between the stones at the tail of a pool in constant expectation of an explosive take.

As the season progresses sea trout are to be found more and more on the gravel runs. These fish can take up position for spawning now that they are losing their blue and silver sheen. In September many of the shallow runs will be populated with dark spotted fish that merge with the river bed. These fish can be agressive and may attack almost any lure but they do not make good eating and do not provide the fight that a fresh run fish can give. They are better left to spawn and the fisherman determined to fish until the end of the season is advised to explore the deeper runs and gullies where cleaner fish may be found.

When autumn salmon fishing, I know I will raise stale sea trout if I fish the gravel runs and so I tend to focus on the channels through the Devon slate where a fresh fish may be lying.

Chapter 4

The Fly

1988 was a pivotal year for my sea trout fishing. My expeditions with the spinning rod had taught me much about the rivers and the nature of the fish that they held. I had my best season ever and succeeded in proving to myself that I could catch these fish when conditions were right. But there were times when low water and bright skies made this approach far from easy. Clear summer rivers left me at a disadvantage when restricted to the spinning rod. I was also beginning to feel that the spinning rod was something of a 'blunt instrument'. Although I was developing the art of selective casting and was not just raking the river I wanted to fish with a little more refinement. Also there were times when I wanted something more of a challenge. I had overcome the first hurdle – I could find and catch fish – I now wanted to catch the more difficult fish.

Having a family and a career kept me busy most of the time and frustratingly, when I did find time for fishing it was during holiday time when the weather was bright and dry. The shrinking rivers made spinning for sea trout something less than unproductive. On such occasions I would sometimes take a light fly rod and wander up the Walkham or Meavy to cast a dry fly for those fast fighting brown trout that inhabit the moorland streams.

Fishing a dry fly on moorland rivers is considerably different from casting a line for chalk stream trout. Dartmoor trout are not particular about the finer points of fly-fishing and it is not always necessary to 'match the hatch'. There are times when Yellow Sallies are hatching through mid summer, and there are sultry evenings when everything alive in the river is throwing itself at black gnats. At these times fishing a close imitation may provoke a rise or two more than fishing something nondescript, but I discovered that the pattern chosen is rarely crucial.

I know that this is contentious and there will be those who are precious about entomology and classic fly fishing but Dartmoor trout are hungry. The little acid streams, while clean and pure, generate relatively poor populations of insect life. Terrestrial insects that fall or get blown into the rivers make up the majority of many fish's diet. I experimented with a variety of flies tied for chalk stream duty and all of them worked. There did not seem to be a fly in my box that could not induce a rise when first dropped onto any likely water of the upper Walkham. The problem with most chalk steam patterns were that they became drowned all too quickly when bobbing down the fast broken water of these rapid waters.
I wanted a fly that had high visibility and good floatation. The trout wanted anything that seemed edible. While I frequently tried old favourites - a Greenwell's Glory or a Black Gnat or even a Blue Quill I began to favour a small Deer Hair Sedge. This would ride high and was taken as readily as any traditional pattern.

On summer evenings when gnats were dancing above the water I would work my way slowly upstream casting to rising fish and raise a fish on every cast. Most of them would be too small to take the size 14 dry fly but it would not stop them trying and occasionally something larger would sip the small fly down. On sunny days when every sensible fish was hugging the bottom a small sedge dropped onto the quiet water over a small deep hole would induce a brown trout to rocket from the depths and hit

DATE	RIVER	BEAT	CONDITIONS
April 1988	Walkham	Merrivale	Low clear water - Southerly breeze blowing up the valley

NOTES

Fishing upstream from Merrivale Newtake – small brown trout would launch themselves at a dry Greenwell's when I could avoid drag. When the fly dragged across the surface fish rose and followed but did not take and the fly became waterlogged. Continually drying the fly became tedious and a size 12 deer hair sedge was substituted. This was accepted with equal enthusiasm by the fish and it proved difficult to sink. Placing the fly remained essential to induce a rise before excessive drag set in but if it did drag and drown the Deer Hair fly floated perfectly after a few false casts.

FISH CAUGHT	8 brown trout to 8oz. All returned	FLY/LURE	Deer hair sedge 12

DATE	RIVER	BEAT	CONDITIONS
August 1987	Walkham	Magpie	Low and clear. Overcast but warm and light

NOTES

Fished upstream from Grenofen Bridge with a dry fly during the evening. Water was low and clear but a steady breeze put a ripple on the water. Took several small browns to a black gnat but changed to a deer hair sedge to fish the faster water. Took several browns to about 8 oz and sea trout took in the run above the Viaduct Pool. This hit the fly as it touched the water and was landed after some jumping – my first sea trout to a dry fly.

FISH CAUGHT	4 browns to 8oz and 1 sea trout 10oz.	FLY/LURE	

DATE	RIVER	BEAT	CONDITIONS
September 1989	Plym		Low clearing. Some overnight rain and the river was carrying a little stain.

NOTES

Late morning – I worked my way up the Cad with a dry fly casting into the small pools with a short line. Several browns below the Dewerstone and two sea trout in the pool adjacent to Lower Cadworthy. The smaller took first and was pulled over the lip and played out in the riffles below. A larger fish took a few casts later and this ran all over the pool. Additional casts produced no interest. I was sure that there was a shoal of sea trout in the pool but I could not induce another to rise. Both sea trout had taken the fly as soon as ot landed. The slightly bulky deer hair dressing does make it plop slightly on the water.

FISH CAUGHT	3 brown trout to 5 oz and 2 sea trout 8oz and 1 lb.	FLY/LURE	DH Sedge 14

the fly hard and fast. I found it paid to 'fish the water' casting to where I expected to find fish. On rare occasions I would rise and sometimes land a sea trout. These events were fortuitous and not planned. Taking a sea trout on a deliberately cast dry fly became a challenge that for a season or two I tackled a little to keenly.

Sea trout are more wary than brown trout and are exceptionally easily spooked. In clear water they often see you long before you see them and an approach from behind and from as low an angle as possible is necessary. Then the cast has to be perfect without excessive false casting or splashing as the line lifts off or drops on the water. Small amounts of drag of the fly appeared not to frighten the fish and could actually provoke a take but once the line started to make ripples the fish would appear to 'quiver' in their lies and at the next cast the bow waves would signal their departure.

My greatest success occurred when walking up a river I found I could place myself below a small waterfall or step in the stream to be almost at eye level with the water surface. Careful fishing of the water towards the head of these small pools, lengthening line a half a metre or so between casts would produce a brown or two and occasionally, and really accidentally, a sea trout. On the rare occasions this happened the sea trout would rise the moment the fly hit the water and take it aggressively and with no hesitation. I have never seen a sea trout rise and inspect a fly like I have seen chalk stream fish rise to a May fly. They spring, seemingly from nowhere, to hit it hard or they sit tight and completely ignore the imitation.

When school peal mass in the shallows at the back of the larger holding pools, I found that some amongst them will rise to a dry fly if it is presented with some finesse. It is hard not to be tempted by large shoals of fish in shallow clear water and offer the fish a lure of some sort. I heard that a young army officer living near me in Horrabridge was taking fish from Grenofen Bridge Pool on a Blue Quill dry fly and so I tried it myself.

It seemed to contradict my theories that sea trout are only likely to respond to the sudden appearance of a prey item. An imitative pattern that drifts slowly over the fish that would tempt a feeding brown trout would be likely to be ignored by the migrant. In the main this proved to be the case. Flies that dropped like thistle down on the lightest of casts and drifted with no drag were ignored by the sea trout only to be gulped down by unseen parr. Occasionally a fly would drop just within a fish's window and it would rise but turn away. Much like a sea trout rises to a spinner seen before it comes into the strike zone. Persistence paid off and I eventually got a fish to take and I kept away from the rest of the school in case there was another that might be tempted but it was to no avail.

A stealthy approach was important but it always is. I tried standing like heron for some twenty minutes, watching and waiting as the fish to become accustomed to my presence. Eventually drawing off some line and make gentle casts half a metre or so a head of the targeted fish – allowing the fly to drift over and past the fish without creating any drag – pause and try another or repeat. I found that if the fly drops just in the right place a settled fish may rise and hit it. But there were no guarantees and experimenting with different flies and drag or no drag produced no discernable improvements. At times I think a little drag when the fly was in the strike zone may have effected a rise but it was difficult to be certain.

I came to the conclusion that sea trout react to an alighting dry fly as they would a lure. A food item suddenly appears in their window and striking range and they instinctively respond. Drifting flies over the fish and giving them plenty of time to view and consider the offering has proved unproductive.

DATE	RIVER	BEAT	CONDITIONS
August 1992	Walkham	Magpie	Low and clear

NOTES

Good shoals of school sea trout in the river and the owner let me fish the Bridge Pool. I started to fish a dry fly over the fish lying at the tail as I have heard that others have had success in this way. A black gnat was initially ignored and although I changed fly a few times I persisted. with the appraoch

I resisted the temptation to cast high up in the centre of the pool but gently fanned out my casts to the left and then back to the right across the resting fish. Althouh I was fishing as gently as I could and the shoal showed no signs of being spooked I was having little success. Twice fish rose to inspect the fly as it landed but turned back without breaking the surface. Eventually well over an hour's patience paid off and one rose and hit the fly with agression. It caused some commotion and although I carried on for another hour I think the fish were disturbed and I could not raise another.

I fished the pool as skillfully as I am able for over three hours. Conditions were good, there was no disturbance and I had just one small peal to show for it. I am not sure that the stories of large catches on the dry fly are not exagerated.

FISH CAUGHT	I sea trout 9oz.	FLY/LURE	Black Gnat size 16

DATE	RIVER	BEAT	CONDITIONS
June 1990	Tavy	Middle	Low and clear

NOTES

It has been low and clear with cold nights – not good for day or night fishing. Tried daytime fishing with a dry fly. I found three large fish in a gully in the middle of a large pool. The low water enabled me to wade out to a rarely exposed rock some ten metres below them but I had to straddle two boulders either side of the remaining channel to get into position to cast. Despite the challenges of my perch I succeeded in raising and hooking a fish of at least four pounds on my first attempt.

The fish immediately leapt and ran for the neck of the pool taking most of my line but having nowhere to run or hide it ran back towards me. Stripping in line to try and keep in contact was suddenly frantic and as I struggled with loops of line the fish shot between my legs and I fell into the river. The fish had slack line and threw the hook. I had wet pants and waders full of water.

FISH CAUGHT		FLY/LURE	Deer Hair Sedge 14

DATE	RIVER	BEAT	CONDITIONS
September 1987	Walkham		Clearing fast

NOTES

I fished with a fly rod on a falling river on the upper Walkham. Small browns and par came regularly to a dry black gnat but none of any size. I decided to try an upstream nymph and continued to catch small browns to a Pheasant Tail nymph. Thinking I needed to get down among the stones I changed to a weighted and began to pick up better browns. At the top of Eggsworthy Weir I took my best Dartmoor brown to date.

FISH CAUGHT	12 brown trout to 1lb 12 oz. – the one fish taken	FLY/LURE	GRHE on a long shank 14

It also proved more worthwhile to target fish that had some company. Small schools of four to six sea trout seemed the most likely to hold a receptive fish. It may be a competitive element as in nature the fish that responds the fastest gets to eat – those who hesitate miss out. On many occasions I found a solitary fish lying in an easily accessible lie that was just too tempting to try for. These always seemed to be asleep until a bad cast or a dragged line sent them dashing upstream and into hiding. Although I kept trying I never had a great deal of success.

Larger fish also seemed less likely to respond to the dry fly and although I know those who have claimed to have taken specimen fish by this method I have hooked very few over a pound. A large sea trout on light tackle is not something for the unskilled and although I have hooked a few I have failed to land any of the larger fish.

Fishing the dry fly on the upper stretches I began, at times to get a little frustrated by the small fish that often presented a nuisance. There were larger fish in the river but their smaller cousins always beat these to the dry fly and so I began to experiment with upstream wet flies and nymphs.

Traditional spider patterns worked well in the fast water as did that West Country classic the 'Half Stone' but again these attracted the under-size browns. Small Pheasant Tail Nymphs brought back through the broken flows had a similar effect but when I tried larger weighted nymphs and started to catch larger browns.

Every 'pot' under a small waterfall seemed to hold a larger resident brown and a heavy fly cast into the cascade and allowed to fall with the flow to wash around and was then retrieved through the bubbles would take the occupants of such pools. This method gave me my two largest Walkham brown trout. Although I have heard of bigger fish I have not seen larger brown trout from Dartmoor.

I tied some Gold Ribbed Hare's Ear nymphs on size 12 long shank hooks with some lead shot, pinched and glued onto the shank. When these were cast upstream into the head of a pool and brought back between the large stones they produced much better trout. My personal record from the River Walkham was a fish of 1lb 12 oz taken on a weighted GRHE. A few years later I repeated this with an identical fish under some roots above Grenofen Bridge. Czech Nymphs on size 12 grub hooks worked just as effectively but were much more time consuming to tie than the GRHE.

The weighted upstream nymph also produced sea trout and I began to fish them through the boulder-strewn runs and the gullies in the slate, with the hope of tempting sea trout. I tied flies with gold beads just behind the hackle and a hare's ear dubbing for a body. Tied on size 10 'gold' head hooks these proved good attractors and good hookers and I began picking up more sea trout. The metal beads were more secure when casting provided an added attraction and were also faster to tie than the Czech patterns.

As I found when spinning, it seemed imperative to surprise the fish with a small fly that looked enticingly like some tasty invertebrate but was rapidly disappearing. It forced an instant decision – hit or miss. The technique was to start at the bottom of a section that was likely to hold fish. To keep out of the river as much as possible and cover the water by casting upstream into a likely run and bringing the fly back just ahead of the current. I tried to imagine the fly travelling with the flow along the bed of the stream rising and falling as I raised the rod as much like a natural as possible. It was necessary to drop the fly in front of the fish to allow it to sink before beginning the retrieve. But long casts up into the heads of pools were to be avoided until all the water below it had been covered first. I was adapting my upstream spinning technique to short line fly-fishing.

DATE	RIVER	BEAT	CONDITIONS
August 2003	Tavy	Middle	Low and clear

NOTES
After a hot day (23C) - early evening fishing upstream through Bertha Run with a Czech Nymph. I could see the fish lying in the runs between the boulders and could cast to targeted fish. Before I spooked the shoal I took 2 fish. Although I could see the fish I could not see the fly and had to gues when it was right to lift the rod. Got it right twice and then I somehow frightened the fish and they shot upstream.

FISH CAUGHT	2 sea trout 1 lb and 1lb 9oz.	FLY/LURE	Czech Nymph - yellow and black Size 14

DATE	RIVER	BEAT	CONDITIONS
July 2003	Tavy	Abbey	

NOTES
Fished a falling river early in the morning with a GRHE gold head on a size 10 hook. Raised a fish in Abbey Pool neck but it did not take. I continued up to JBs Run and took a matching pair of sea trout close to the bank. Returning to the pool I decided to try the lie where I raised the first fish with little optimism. Second cast was taken by a grilse which took some landing on the trout rod.

FISH CAUGHT	2 sea trout both 2lb 6 oz. 1 salmon 5lb 12 oz	FLY/LURE	GRHE Gold Head 10

DATE	RIVER	BEAT	CONDITIONS
May 1993	Tavy		River up some colour

NOTES
Fished downstream with a small weighted treble (Bluebottle dressing size 14). One fish took in the Long Pool as the fly landed. A second fish took in the Sand Pool at the tail as the fly drifted into near bank. Two other fish took of subsequent casts as the fly drifted into the same eddy and was then drawn away but neither landed.

FISH CAUGHT	2 sea trout 2lb 4oz and 2lb 8 oz	FLY/LURE	Bluebottle size 14

I experimented extensively with purely imitative nymph patterns but I am never sure if the fish were deceived by the pattern or by its delivery. In short summer spates a weighted 'Wooley Worm' tied on a long shank size 10 has taken sea trout when drifted and bounced through a run. Initially this was meant to catch those fish that had taken slugs but when it worked it caught those with empty bellies.

I have also taken a fish by dropping a Czech Nymph under some oaks where the sea trout taken was bloated with fallen caterpillars but the fish concerned may have taken anything that appeared in its window. There is no way of knowing and although I occasionally catch fish that have recently taken natural prey, with the above exception, I have never caught another fish that has consumed anything resembling the pattern that took it. Fishing imitative patterns for sea trout on West Country river has its limitations and I now consider my flies as lures and fish them accordingly. The advantage of an imitative pattern lies in its ability to assume some of the camouflage of the natural in that it is less likely to be seen until it reaches the strike zone.

Fishing the weighted fly is much improved when there is a little colour in the water and it is not so important to be downstream of the fish. Then cross stream casts can explore the channels and eddies with greater control. When the rain has stopped, the river is dropping and it becomes too clear for downstream casts it can be perfect for the up and across 'gold head'. Again I find it pays to fish the water and allow the nymph to trundle through likely or known lies – lifting the rod tip now and again to lift the fly off the bottom and induce a take. This is very much like the Czech technique but with an increased distance between you and the fish.

Close to the bottom the fish's window is restricted by stones and rocks and drifting debris. A weighted nymph drifting with the current close to the bottom will not be seen until it is quite close and probably well within the sea trout's strike zone. If within this zone the fly appears to move up and away from the fish its instinct takes over and it is unable to resist a strike. It is not a method recommended for a high and full river but when the water is returning to summer levels but is still carrying peat stain it can be far more productive than spinning.

Unlike chalk stream nymph fishing the sea trout fisherman will be unable to see the fish and it is very rare that I have been able to cast to specific targets. It pays to have knowledge of the river. My years of combing the river with a spinning rod under the tutorage of the old-timers taught me where I would be likely to find fish. In low water I made close examinations of the river bottom and used photographs to help memorise the underwater terrain. When dark and coloured I can use this knowledge to visualise the channels and the snags and try to place my flies to best advantage.

My efforts with the dry fly suggested that sea trout are often attracted by the fall of the fly onto the water. Another club member who often fishes a weighted fly has remarked that, "it has to make a plop". The added weight of under body lead or a brass bead gives it the additional mass required to make some noise and ripple on entering the stream. This attracts the fish's attention and as soon as the fly make that little splash it will rise and take it but it has to fall within the fish's strike zone. This calls for accurate casting and knowledge of the water but is immensely satisfying. Those little pockets of quiet water on the edge of a stream in spate are the places to try this approach and can often save an otherwise fruitless day when the water is opaque and all other methods fail.

The fish will be facing into the stream and its window may stretch to a metre, two or three depending upon the clarity of the water and its

DATE	RIVER	BEAT	CONDITIONS
July 2005	Tavy	Middle	No significant rise but carrying some colour- light ale

NOTES

Arrived to find Wolfie and guest spinning with small plugs and enthusing about the fish they had raised. It appeared that a shoal of peal were passing through. How many had they caught? Well none actually landed. How many hooked? Several hit the lure! When they moved off to fish upstream I fished down where they had been spinning with the fly rod. I was not optimistic but immediately I was into a fish which was landed and then another. In all I hooked and landed 5 in less than an hour and left the river with a good brace for supper.

FISH CAUGHT	5 landed - 2 sea trout taken 1 lb 2 oz. One fish was heavily spotted.	FLY/LURE	Gold head size 10

depth. (NB If lying in one of those eddies at the shoulder of a pool while facing into the flow a sea trout could be looking down the river.) The strike zone is unlikely to exceed a metre or so and a fish is unlikely to attack anything seen outside this limit. Ideally we want the fly to land on the edge of the strike zone where the fish's attention may be grabbed by the sudden discovery that a potential food item is within range but may be escaping. Feeding instinct takes over and it attacks

When the river is running clear the traditional downstream wet fly approach has rarely proved productive. Traditional wet flies will take the occasional salmon and small patterns will lure brown trout but the sea trout are particularly shy. It is difficult to fish, fine and far off' on the fast streams that tumble from riffle to pool down steep inclines. Back casts are often limited and when forced to fish a short line it puts you very close to the quarry. Occasionally I find I can use natural cover or fast water to shield me from the fish's eyes. I sometimes try to drift a fly over a lie from a place of hiding but on wide runs, tails and glides the fish sees a fisherman working downstream well before it sees the fly. There is also the problem that in clear water the fish sees the fly well before it reaches striking range. The only chances are created

when a wet fly can drift up to a sea trout that is shielded by under water obstructions and unaware of its approach. When the fly suddenly appears from around a boulder sometimes it can sometimes trigger the right response.

In coloured water things are different and a wet fly fished down and across can produce exciting sport. Fishing down all the runs by casting across and down and varying the angle with the speed of the flow will catch a few fish unawares and result in takes. It may be a sea trout, brown trout or salmon. I try to give known lies a little extra care and perhaps an extra cast or two. I often try dropping the rod to let the fly drift and sink and raising as the fly passes through a known lie to induce a rise. Retrieving a 'handful' of line every so often as the fly swings across the current can have a similar effect.

Sea trout do not seem to want a static lure and will not take a fly that has come to the end of its arc and is hanging motionless. As the cast fishes out it is important to retrieve line to keep the fly on the move. If the fly swings into the near bank and then moves forward as a couple of feet of line is stripped a fish will often take. I am never sure if a fish has been following the fly across the stream and attacked as it changes speed and direction or if it was a fish resting by the bank who saw a moving object swing into its strike zone. I suspect the latter.

Fly selection is important and I am mindful of the need to select a pattern that gives the fish the impression of a prey item but is not going to be seen before it gets close enough to strike.

I carry more flies than I ever need and admire those who can restrict themselves to a few patterns and sizes all season. They probably do a lot more fishing and less peering into fly boxes trying to choose what to tie on next. In very heavy water I tend to fish a small copper tube with a simple dressing of pearl mylar with blue hair wing. In low but dark water I used to favour a small treble with lead foil under a body of blue tinsel, a fly I called the 'Bluebottle' but now prefer a single with a silver or brass bead for weight. As the water continues to drop I reduce size of lure and select simple patterns tied on salmon doubles and trout singles. Patterns include Black Pennel, Silver March Brown and Spider hybrids. The clearer the water becomes the more naturalistic the pattern chosen. The sea trout is not stuffy and patterns do not have to be exact. When I can see the bottom at a depth of greater than a metre I sometimes turn around and work upstream with my weighted patterns.

The fly much more versatile and allows me to cover the fish with greater control of depth and speed. I can adjust patterns to suit conditions and take greater risks in trying to cover a lie.

Losing a fly I have tied myself is a minor irritation compared to losing a spinner or plug that may have cost several pounds. I will shrug and snap off a snagged fly but will wade a stream and climb a tree to retrieve an expensive plug. (I will also wade streams and climb trees to avoid leaving lengths of trailing nylon). It is irritating to lose the last of a successful pattern when nothing similar is in the box, but it gives me an excuse to take out the tying kit after dinner and spend an enjoyable couple of hours tying replacements. It also creates another opportunity to invent a few new ones.

Fishing a fly up or down a beat takes much more time and much more effort than spinning. It is more rewarding and it is usually more productive but it is slower and less water is covered. It is like comparing the enjoyment of a long French lunch with grabbing a sandwhich on the move. There are times when I want to snatch a little fishing but am constrained by the time. When I am stealing an hour or so from a hectic schedule I am as likely as not to be indolent and reach for the spinning rod to dash out and hit a few of my favourite hot spots, to enjoy a few casts while conditions hold good, before hurrying back to other duties.

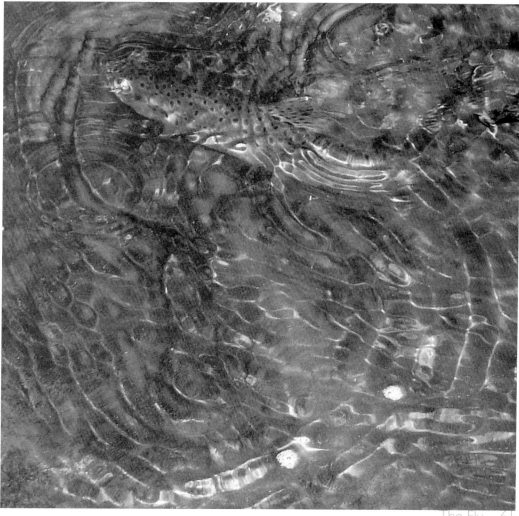

When I have the luxury of a good spell of time - a whole morning, afternoon or evening the fly rod will be the first choice regardless of conditions. After dark there is no question – it is the fly rod every time.

Fishing should be unhurried. It needs to be slow, steady but purposeful. The beat is walked, the air enjoyed and the cast is measured. Spinning can be too frantic and bait fishing is too static. Fishing the fly, I feel is undoubtably the most rewarding way to fish.

Chapter 5

The Night

When darkness falls it brings distinct changes to the sea trout's environment and these changes can be very helpful to the fisherman. Darkness also creates some obvious difficulties, but with a little planning these can be overcome. On balance, with the fading of the light the sea trout's window is restricted and the skilful angler has a considerable advantage. As night comes to a sea trout river it brings opportunities for the most exciting fishing to be experienced.

Darkness makes it much more difficult for the fish and the fisherman to see each other. An angler who has studied the river and its lies will be able to locate fish and take up positions where casts can be made over holding water. The fisherman's eyes will adapt and if not dazzled by careless use of a torch will be able to maintain sufficient night vision to place controlled casts over fish on all but the darkest nights. The sea trout has amazing eyesight but is hampered by reflections from the surface. Once total darkness has arrived it is unlikely to see a human who keeps below the skyline and avoids sudden movements. This enables a stealthy angler to approach the fish and get to within (sometimes) easy casting range.

The approach most commonly adopted at night is the traditional down and across wet fly technique. This is not technically demanding but requires a little practice to avoid tangles in the dark. It is worth trying casting with a blindfold or with eyes closed if new to fly fishing in the dark, before going to the river. Each season before the sea trout fishing gets under way I practice my casting over popular lies while daytime fishing. I take up my favourite stands and with a relaxed gentle rhythm make short

and gentle casts and once the knack returns I extend my line until I am covering the lies. I get rusty during the close season and can get into a terrible tangle on the first few nights I venture out. Practice for me is a necessity but these training sessions take place when there is unlikely to be any sea trout fishing on that night.

Fishing at night with a fly rod enables the lies to be covered carefully and methodically. The lure can be placed within the fish's strike zone with control and take it by surprise. The reduced light makes this easier and a fly that suddenly comes out of the darkness to sweep past the fish's nose will trigger aggressive instincts. But operating in the dark is not that easy and sea trout, as I have tried to express, are extremely nervous fish and are very easily spooked. Even in complete darkness clumsy casting, splashing or thumping around with heavy feet will reverse the advantage.

Creeping around softly has never been my forte and in the dark I stumble and easily lose my balance. Walking stony, root strewn and overgrown riverbanks needs care in the daytime, in the dark every step seems to spring a trap of some sort. Despite my best efforts I frequently slip and trip over wet and loose stones as I am approaching the water. Leaping fish distract and excite me. My efforts to slow down and travel carefully are confounded by excitement. Try as I will, I do create more noise than I would like. But as the season progresses I get back into the routine and with some effort I can maintain sufficient discretion to take a fish or two and remain in one piece.

In the daytime I can walk along the bank casting as I go but at night I find this impossible

DATE	RIVER	BEAT	CONDITIONS
July 2005	Tavy	Middle	Low, clear with half moon just above the skyline. High thin cloud 17C

NOTES

Arrived at 10.00pm with at least an hour to pass before fishing could begin but found Mr Bizzie had made a premature start. He compounded his folly by frequently checking his flies with a powerful torch. I watched and waited until it was fully dark and by which time he had arrived at the tail of the pool fishless.

With his permission I started well below him on water that had not been fished as yet that night. A rising moon was providing some light and so I remained a rod's length back from the water and began to cast into the shadows. Almost immediately I was into a peal that was beached and bagged. Next cast I had a violent pull but the fish was lost after cart wheeling around the pool. I continued to cover the lies but having disturbed the water no further takes came and I moved upstream.

Looping up behind my fellow fisherman I continued on the water that he had covered nearly two hours before. It was now as dark as it was going to get. Keeping between the moon beams I had much more cover and the water was now rested. I was soon into a good fish that leapt twice and came unstuck. At the next stand I took and landed a good sized 'schoolie'. With a brace in the bag I moved on down to exchange notes with the other fisherman. He had had one pull but his bag remained empty – I left him to continue alone.

FISH CAUGHT	2 sea trout 12 oz and 1lb 2oz	FLY/LURE	Size 10 Black and Silver

without slipping or tripping. I find that I have to adapt my approach and where in daylight I would continue to fish as I made my way along the bank, in the dark I try to behave sensibly and completely reel in, or at least shorten line after fishing from one stand. I then feel my way down river a few metres and begin again. This inevitably slows up the fishing but it cuts down on the noise, the disturbance and the tangles. Ultimately it probably avoids wasting time dealing with snagged and knotted casts. It is also safer and enables me to cast with greater care and control. I can keep a low profile when moving from stand to stand as I can crouch and keep my head down below the skyline when I do not have to worry about trailing lines.

A fish that can feed in the dark is armed with exceptional eyesight and this makes it aware of movement that may be invisible to humans in the same light conditions. As I have said the fisherman has the advantage but sudden movements against even a dark sky will scare fish and 'put them down'. A colleague armed with a 'night sight' has watched the movement of fish from a bridge while I fished from the bank. He noted that the fish moved away from bank as I approached despite it being close to total darkness. While I remained relatively still and below the skyline, the fish drifted back into position.

The fishes' initial reaction may have been in response to the visual sensation of my appearing on the bank or it could have been the sound and vibration, created by my blundering. I have no way of knowing but I try to move slowly and deliberately. Despite this I know that others sharing a beat with me at night have been able to hear my stumbling several hundred yards away. (I wish to make a public apology for these disturbances - which I do try to minimise.) I always try to remain at least a rod length back from the waters edge wherever possible and wade only when there is no other way of covering the lies.

Normal conversation does not seem to affect the fish, and as far as I am aware of there is no need for whispering, but talking does inhibit concentration on the job in hand. In the dark I need to be able to take in every sound coming from the river and its surroundings to make sense of what is going on. Listening to the river helps give me a sense of direction. Staring into the darkness and listening to the roar of the weir downstream or the burbling of the current over the rock above I can sense my place in my surroundings without reliance upon visual references. Casting in uninterrupted silence I can hear the fish move to the surface and the lure hit the water. I can tell if they were close or metres apart. A flick of the leaves on the far bank as I cast indicates I need to shorten line. Unnecessary chatter takes this focus away and the results are often frustrating. That is not to say I appreciate some social conversation while waiting for darkness and an exchange of 'notes' when swapping places or when the fishing has ended is useful and very enjoyable but once fishing in under way silence is recommended. Sharing a beat with someone who knows how to enjoy silent companionship is a pleasure but alas a rare one.

Often I am asked to take friends, acquaintances or new members to the river at night. This can be delightful and I have in the past benefited from the generosity of others but on such expeditions there is a need for constant conversation – explanation and sometimes instruction. When you cannot see faces and expressions talk is important but this seems to create a barrier between the environment and me. Inevitably there are fewer fish caught and I often worry about my companions' lack of success or entertainment.

I have other fishermen friends who, despite their obvious desire to partake of the 'cream of game angling' will not venture out at night alone. They would accompany others or me, but when this is not possible they stick to

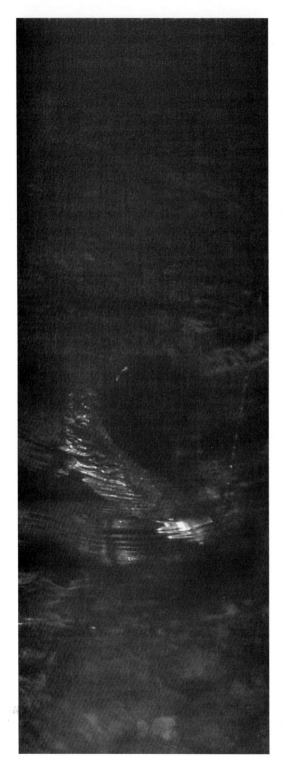

DATE	RIVER	BEAT	CONDITIONS
July 1988	Walkham	Magpie	Low clear river – high thin cloud 12 C

NOTES
I hooked a good fish an hour after dark but the cast became entangled in a stray branch (floating in the stream). Eventually the fish tired but the branch remained attached and I pulled both towards me. I subsequently found that the branch was preventing me from netting it cleanly. Twigs were also catching in the bottom and this stopped me beaching the combined branch and fish. Reluctantly I put a torch on the combination. The fish remained still for a moment but then began to thrash violently and shook itself free. I continued to 1.00 am but did not raise another fish. I regretted using the torch - had I lost the fish by blundering blindly I may not have put off other potential takers

FISH CAUGHT	2 sea trout 1lb and 1lb 2oz	FLY/LURE	Size 10 Special

DATE	RIVER	BEAT	CONDITIONS
July 2001	Tavy	Middle	Low clear 15C

NOTES
Young Flasher, one of the new members became tangled and switched on a torch to recover his cast. He was considerate and moved back fr,om the river so that his light would not affect the fish but I could clearly see it and couldn't resist trying to see what he was doing. Although a hundred metres or so off my night vision was affected and whilst I could just see where my line was landing prior to the light going on I now could discern any landmarks. It took a full twenty minutes to feel comfortable again and get my rhythm back. Nothing was lost but it was a reminder that use of the torch is best avoided

FISH CAUGHT	2 sea trout 1lb and 1lb 2oz	FLY/LURE	Size 10 Special

DATE	RIVER	BEAT	CONDITIONS
August 1989	Walkham	Magpie	Low Clear

NOTES
Many fish showing and I had two 'missed' takes in quick succession in the shallows above the bridge pool. A few minutes later a car passed over the bridge and I lost my night sight when its lights tailed away. I subsequently lost my rhythm and the next cast landed over the moving fish in a heap. Fish stopped leaping and all was quiet until midnight when I fish began splashing in the run. I missed a fish in the corner above the bridge and about 20 minutes later had another take in the same place. This one put up a good fight but was eventually beached on the gravel. Arrived home at 1.00am.

FISH CAUGHT	1 sea trout 2lb 4oz	FLY/LURE	Size 10 Sinfoil Fry

daytime fishing. I feel a little guilty and joke with them about being afraid of the dark but it is possibly good sense and I think I am probably behaving irresponsibly. I would like to invite them to join me more often but I need to fish alone even though there are obvious dangers. I suggest my approach with some reluctance and recommend others to exercise extreme caution if following my example.

In order to fish effectively in the dark the sea trout fisherman accompanied or otherwise needs to be well organised (I wish) and become familiar with the pools to be fished and the access to them. I can usually deal with wind knots and tangles by feel but I these days I need a torch to change flies. When this is necessary I back away from the river to keep the artificial light off the water. A red filter helps a great deal to reduce the effect this has on my 'night vision'. Without the filter, it takes me some time to regain my ability to make out the landmarks. I find stopping, closing my eyes and listening intently for about five minutes helps.

I have noticed that looking at lights others are using, even if they are a couple of hundred metres away, also affects my ability to see into the dark. Even the stars on a bright night can reduce my night sight. A wide brimmed hat helps to shield my eyes from such distractions but I always do my best to shield others (and the river) from the light when I am forced to switch on my torch. If I need light I walk away from the river, turn my back and drop to my knees in the handiest clump of vegetation. I may also use a torch when leaving for home up the path but if someone else is still fishing I try not to switch it on until I am well away from the river. Putting a torch on the water, although tempting at times, certainly frightens the fish and this must be avoided.

It is important to cast gently and avoid dropping the line with any excessive splashing. I use the lightest line that will handle the range of lures

I use with control and try to execute perfect casts every time. There is rarely any need to stretch for distance and there is no need to rush. Fishing at night needs to be a relaxed, almost meditative activity with nothing hurried and nothing forced, just careful rhythmic motions. When casting well I feel optimistic and happy but this can sometimes be a challenge on wild untamed beats. On many a night something has distracted me and I have lost my rhythm and cast badly. The cast has landed in a heap on the water creating disturbance and knots. Disturbing the stream over the fish, especially on the flat water of a calm pool does nothing to induce the fish to come to the fly and continuing to flog that section of water after a bad cast is a waste of time. I now rest the pool or that section of it, check and repair my cast, returning to fish those lies at least 30 minutes or so later if this happens.

A high degree of familiarity can be beneficial to fish a pool effectively in the dark. I am fortunate in that the pools I regularly fish at night have also been fished a great deal in the daylight (for over twenty years). This has served me well but the knowledge has been gained through fishing the river when conditions dictated that daytime fishing was the only option. Those who are familiar with the sport leave sea trout pools alone during the day if there is any likelihood of them being fished at night. If some day-time fishing is required and the river is low and clear, the less accessible and least fished places are sought out. Only a complete novice fishes the sea trout pools while waiting for darkness to come.

If I want to check how a fly is fishing or practise casting while waiting for dark I go to a run that will not be fished and these days I rarely carry out any daylight pre-fishing reconnaissance. Although many recommend it I prefer to keep away from the chosen pools as much as possible to allow the fish to settle. I have noted that pools disturbed in the daytime by

DATE	RIVER	BEAT	CONDITIONS
August 1998	Tavy	Middle	Low clear no moon

NOTES

Arrived at the pool at dusk to find Derek, a new member spinning through the run. He waved cheerfully to me and carried on. He eventually returned to the seat and picked up his fly rod and set out to cover the water again. After about an hour he stopped and asked me why I was not fishing. With some control I explained that it was my habit to wait for full darkness and not to go near the water before dark, let alone fish it. I tried not to display any impatience but he huffed and quoted the practice on another river where his approach was standard and then went back to the water.

Fishing water that had not been disturbed I managed a brace from the Flats. Returning to the main pool I found Derek complaining of no fish and preparing to leave for bed. I said nothing and sat down and listened to him sound off and then go. The best water had been well thrashed but out of curiosity I gave it a try. I fished as carefully as I could without a touch before I returned to the (un fished) Flats where I immediately hooked and landed another schoolie.

FISH CAUGHT	3 sea trout 14oz -1lb.	FLY/LURE	Size 10 Special

DATE	RIVER	BEAT	CONDITIONS
July 2004	Tavy	Middle	Very low and clear with hidden moon 15C

NOTES

The pool I intended to fish was occupied by someone who had started early and so I took the long walk downstream to a quieter stretch. Once fully dark I began to fish the pool and found a shoal of fish. For half an hour I had terrific sport with many takes, five fish hooked and two landed. With a brace in the bag I returned to the main pool where the other fisherman was bemoaning the lack of fish in the river!

FISH CAUGHT	2 sea trout 1 lb 12 oz and 2lb 2oz.	FLY/LURE	Size 10 Special

DATE	RIVER	BEAT	CONDITIONS
August 2003	Tavy	Middle	Low and clear but intermittent misty rain. 15C

NOTES

Light intermittent rain all day had kept trippers away from the river and despite it being a weekend there had probably been little disturbance. Fishing proved quite remarkable. Fish were not showing a great deal but I had many missed takes, I landed five fish and lost three and made it to the pub before closing time. Had I wished to fish on I am sure I could have landed another five.

FISH CAUGHT	5 sea trout 12oz – 1lb 4oz	FLY/LURE	Size 10 Half Silver Size 10 Black Fly

swimmers, children throwing stones or the dreaded 'stick throwing dog walkers' do not produce any takes until much later than I would expect, Pools that have usually produced a rise or two by 10.30 on a mild night may not see any movement to the fly until after midnight if there has been any previous disturbance, if at all. Inexperienced sea trout fishermen who start too early will have the same detrimental effect.

In his book , 'A Trout Angler's Notebook', H.S. Joyce complains about some anglers who lived on the Tavy near to one of the beats I fish. He claims they would keep a lookout for approaching sea trout fishermen and dash out with a spinning rod and fish over the best taking water before they arrived in order to put off the fish. Thankfully someone far more sporting now owns the house.

I have never experienced deliberate disruption of the kind reported by Joyce but it is not unknown to encounter an over-enthusiastic new member. One who has experienced different customs on other rivers may be found spinning through the sea trout pools before dark. I am sure there are other rivers where the fish become used to disturbance and are less affected but the Tavy sea trout are extremely wary and need to be pursued with the utmost guile and stealth. Only the naïve or the selfish adopt such practices on the West Country rivers.

Most of those who I regularly fish with agree upon the time to begin fishing but new members to the club and visitors often bring other ideas. On some rivers it seems to be the practice to begin as soon as the bats are flying. While I appreciate bats over the water as a good omen they often begin flying well before I feel it is time to begin fishing. I leave the sea trout runs and pools alone until I am unable to recognise colours – when everything becomes grey and I am unable to see any colours ('when you cannot see the green of the grass as a

famous West Country gillie often advises'!). Another good guide is being unable to see anyone standing on the opposite bank. The fisherman who starts too early will catch the occasional fish, but runs the greater chance of spoiling the fishing for himself and for others. Fishing before dark allows the sea trout to see the flies before they come within striking range. A rise and take is unlikely but the fish's feeding instinct may have been unsettled. Subsequent sights of a lure will not reawaken an instinct that has been partly aroused and suppressed. Patience is rewarded!

There is public access to much of the water I fish and this causes some difficulty at the peak of the sea trout season. Children want to play in the water and people have to throw sticks for their dogs to swim out and retrieve. These activities have an effect on sea trout. Brown trout may appreciate the food items that are disturbed by the water sport but sea trout just hide. When the activities cease they are likely to leave the depths and seek out quieter places where they are most commonly taken. The problem increases during weekends and holidays and I catch fewer fish on these occasions. If I do catch fish they are taken much later in the night and now, if I know my favourite pool has been disturbed by trippers I do not begin to fish until one hour after it is fully dark and usually do not get a take until midnight.

Strangely, otters swimming through a pool during darkness do not disrupt sea trout fishing as much as may be thought. Probably more often than I realise an otter will pass me while I am fishing. Several times each season I see the reflections of the stars shaking on the water, I sense bow waves moving up stream, and see the dark head of an otter circling around me. Several times when I have been wading an otter has decided to swim up to investigate me and has swirled under my rod tip. When I have been unaware of the otter's presence and out of the

DATE	RIVER	BEAT	CONDITIONS
July 2002	Tavy	Lower Beat	Low clear water. High cloud 17C

NOTES

Sitting at the head of Sand Pool waiting for darkness I saw an otter swimming through the run below. I remained where I was and watched bow waves from the rival fisherman work their way towards me. Now and again the head of the otter appeared. Quite soon I thought I was about to have a close encounter with this shy and quite rare animal. but it turned away and waded onto the adjacent gravel bank. I lost sight of it in the shadows but could hear it scampering on the stones and crunching on the bones of a fish - not a sea trout I hoped. While I enjoyed the experience I was a little concerned it may be detrimental to the fishing and thought about moving. But I soon heard it slide back into the water and sensed it moving upstream. Once it was fully dark I started to fish and took two sea trout right against the bank where the otter had enjoyed its supper and another in the run below.

FISH CAUGHT	2 sea trout 2lb and 1lb 8oz	FLY/LURE	10 Orange Special

DATE	RIVER	BEAT	CONDITIONS
June 1999	Tavy	Middle	Low and clear, cloud cover 13C

NOTES

Fishing down The Run a fish kept showing adjacent to the narrow gully. I covered it possibly ten times, changed flies and tried again but could not interest it and so moved on having probably given it too much attention. . I fished until midnight in the main pool with no success and saw little movement of fish and so returned to The Narrows - it had been rested for nearly two hours. Second cast and I was into a fish and this was walked upstream, netted and bagged. Returning to the gully I took another in exactly the same place

FISH CAUGHT	2 sea trout 2lb 4oz and 14 oz	FLY/LURE	Size 10LS Special

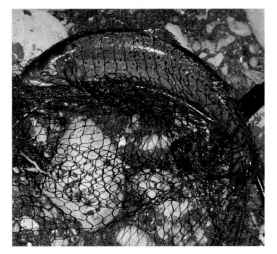

dark water a large animal appears with a great splash I have been temporarily terrified. But once it has sensed the human presence it will not stay and after it has gone and once I have regained some composure, fish will show and may be taken.

I arrive at the pools I intend to fish about an hour before it is dark and enjoy the time of waiting and watching until the time comes to cast a line. I usually set up my rod/s before I leave home and arrive at the river fully prepared. I then sit and watch as one set of wildlife goes to sleep and other set wakes up. As the sea trout start splashing I note their locations. Eventually bats and owls replace the swallows and the martins. I keep well back from the river and do not make an approach until it is quite dark. Once the time has arrived I circle around to the head of the pool and begin fishing the fast run into the pool. My typical approach as it gets darker is to work my way slowly and methodically towards the belly of the pool arriving at the tail when it is darkest of all.

I lengthen line or take a step so that every cast covers new ground sweeping the known taking water in arcs that increase in diameter by 20 or so centimeter. The sections where I have rarely found fish I tend to hurry through and the hot spots receive more attention but I have found it unproductive to repetitively cast over one lie. If there is no response by the third cast it is better to continue down and return to that location later. If I catch a fish I try to play it out upstream, net it, bag or release and begin fishing again a couple of metres or so above the spot where the fish took and pass over the lie once again. It is surprising how often another fish can be taken from the same lie or on the next cast down if the hooked fish is walked upstream and netted as quietly as possible.

When several club members are fishing the same pools we usually agree at dusk where each of us will start to fish. The first to arrive is invariably given the first choice. We begin at our allotted place and progress down the pool towards the tail when the lowest loops back to the top and follow down once again. This may be repeated several times in a night. It works very well and everyone gets a fair chance of a fish. Although I prefer to fish alone I find that I often fish better when I have some competition. I am unable to hurry through to the hot spot' and I fish with far greater care and effort.

When fishing alone I work my way down through the pool trying to cover fresh ground with each cast. Once the pool has been fished through I either move to a new pool or start at the top again and work through the pool once again. As long as it was fished quietly and carefully the first time and it was fully dark when fishing began the second time through a pool is often the more productive. It may be a change in temperature or, more likely, it is that much darker.

Fishing statically from one stand is much less productive but there are times when options are limited. When fishing in company it is unacceptable to hog one spot as each should move down the pool in procession. If there is no alternative continued light casting over a travelling lie can produce a fish or sometimes two. I used to regularly fish the run into a deep holding pool below a bridge. The bridge marked the end of the beat and the pool itself was in private hands and was not often available to me. When it was completely dark fish would move up under the bridge and onto the shallow gravel run above. The taking zone was just a couple of metres long but slow gentle casting over this area could produce a fish or two once it was really dark. It was important not to cast down under the bridge as the fish would get lined and become spooked. By just covering the fish with the nylon cast it was possible to avoid frightening them and eventually patience would be rewarded as a taking fish moved into the zone.

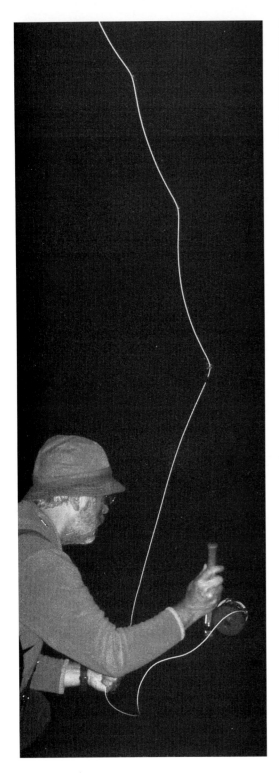

DATE	RIVER	BEAT	CONDITIONS
August 1987	Walkham	Magpie	Low, clear warm and overcast

NOTES

Fishing the run into the bridge pool after dark I became distracted by the fish jumping in the pool and cast down under the bridge. Fished on to gone midnight with no takes. The following night I tried again and resisted the temptation to cast to fish showing through the bridge. One hour after dark I raised three fish over the gravel ridge above the bridge and landed one.

FISH CAUGHT	1 sea trout 3lb 6oz to	FLY/LURE	Size 10 Mallard and Silver

DATE	RIVER	BEAT	CONDITIONS
July 2005	Tavy	Middle	River low and clear, full moon below the skyline. 18C – 15C

NOTES

A bright moon but fortunately it was not shining directly on the water. I fished shadows but with no success. I thought about leaving early but stayed on doggedly. There was another fishing the pool and I knew if I left early and he took a good bag I would be teased for the rest of the season.
Fish did not come onto the take until after midnight then sport was fast and furious. The moon had risen but there was sufficient shadow over some of the hot spots. I took a good 2lb fish at the tail and 4 schoolies from the neck of the pool in the shadows between the moonbeams (lost 2 raised more). Each fish took as soon as the flies were 'fishing' and with a couple of feet of the landing spot Gaining rapid contact with the flies after each cast proved essential.

FISH CAUGHT	5sea trout 1 – 2lb, 1 1-5lb 9oz, 1 –1lb, 2- 12oz	FLY/LURE	Size 10 half Silver or Blue Special

Repetitive casting over one lie prevents any surprise to resident fish and these are unlikely to take. Stands that can remain productive throughout a night are those through which fish move but it is always better to move on and try to locate undisturbed fish if at all possible.

The darker the night the slower I find I need to work my flies. In the 'pitch black' of a cloudy night with no moon I try to drift my flies through the lies as slow as possible. On lighter nights the fly needs to travel a little faster so that the fish has less time to respond. I fish much as I would if I were fishing in the day in clearing water. On most nights I allow my flies to swing around with the current sometimes trying to impart a gentle sink and draw action. I follow the fly around with the rod, allowing it to drift and then retrieve about 20 – 30 cm, drift again and retrieve. If this produces no response I will try an almost continuous retrieve of slow gentle pulls or alternatively allow the fly to just drift with the current. I have never had any success with a fast 'stripping' retrieve although I know many recommend it.

I try to get my flies fishing as soon as they hit the water. As the cast finishes I gather slack line and immediately ensure I have contact with the flies. It is easy, especially when sport is slow, to get into bad habits of casting and then taking one's time at sorting out the free line and taking up the slack. Sea trout very often respond to the flies falling onto the surface and will hit them before they have travelled a metre. A laid back or novice angler can still be recovering loops of line at this stage and misses the take. This became very evident when I was fishing a pool with another fisherman during a light summer night. There was a low moon and I was fishing the shadows at the head and tail of the pool and adjacent runs. Fish did not begin to take until after midnight but shortly after I found two taking places and before long had five fish in the net. Fish kept coming, I had

doubled my usual limit and had more but when I decided I had better call it a night I found my companion was fishless! I was surprised and immediately suggested he try the places where I had been successful. I guided him to the taking places against the far bank at the head of the pool.

With little difficulty he was able to drop his cast into the taking zone and his flies were passing over fish that just before had been fighting over my flies. Alas nothing seemed to be taking but I could just make out movement of moonlight over the water that suggested the fish were rising to his flies. Again and again he cast with no results and so I stood beside him to try and comprehend what was happening. He was dropping his flies perfectly but then stopping to arrange the loose loops of line left over from the cast. By the time this had been completed and he had taken up the slack of his line the flies were beyond the very narrow taking zone and were into the moonlight.

Sometimes a fish will respond to the surface disturbance the fly makes upon landing and when it breaks the surface as it is being recast. On many occasions I have been taken by surprise by a fish that takes at my feet as I am lifting the flies from the water. I think they may have been attracted by the surface disturbance. A wake fly can take advantage of this characteristic. A muddler or popper will provoke a series of aborted takes as it swings across the pool. Pools that seemed devoid of life may wake up when the wake fly is dragged across the surface and fish swirl and splash at the lure. It creates a great deal of excitement and the occasional positive take that can sometimes produce the only fish of the night. But it does not always work and I am always worried that a wake fly will cause too much disturbance and put the fish down so I am reluctant to use it except when all else has failed (and I really would like a fish). If no one else fishing the pool I will sometimes try a wake

DATE	RIVER	BEAT	CONDITIONS
August 1999	Tavy	Lower	Low and clear – overcast no moon 16C

NOTES

Fished through the run and main pool without a take. I had been casting welll and had not put down fish by splashing or stumbling through the water. I had not had one pull and was feeling a little dispondent. Fish were showing but would not rise to the fly.

I had to be up early the next day and was about to give up but decided to fish through the tail of the pool with a muddler. This was taken savagely on the third cast. After a good fight the fish was netted and bagged. I continued for another half an hour but could not raise a second fish.

FISH CAUGHT	1 sea trout 3lb 8 oz	FLY/LURE	8 Muddler Minnow. LS Size 8

DATE	RIVER	BEAT	CONDITIONS
May 2000	Tavy	Middle	Low cloud 11C

NOTES

Fishing with the General on the middle beat for two hours after dark with no action what so ever. A few fsih were showing which gave a little hope but there were no takes. Eventually I heard the other rod's reel singing as he hooked a fish, two hundred metres below. Instantly I had a take and was into a battle with a large fish. Alas mine was lost at the net. but my friend landed his fish, a fresh sea trout of over 5lb. Both of us fished on until the early hours with no further action.

FISH CAUGHT	1 lost	FLY/LURE	Special Size10

DATE	RIVER	BEAT	CONDITIONS
July 2006	Tavy	Middle	River low and clear, No moon, cloud and very dark 15C

NOTES

Conditions were perfect and I had the pool to myself. Fished without distractions as well as I can but had no takes. Fish had been showing since dusk and this motivated me to keep going. At 12.30 I began to fish the neck of the pool again and the point fly was taken by a lively peal. The fish was netted and bagged and a few casts later I was into another fish which proved to be a little bigger.

I subsequently heard on the grapevine that two other anglers fishing the next beat down had both taken fish at 12 .30 after fishing hard from dusk and continued until dawn with no further sport.

FISH CAUGHT		FLY/LURE	Size 12 Black Special

fly before leaving for home and this has saved the day on many occasions. Never have I taken more

Changes in the light clearly effect the mood of the sea trout. These are creatures that habitually feed at night and the coming of darkness must be akin to the ringing of the dinner bell. Although the fish probably feel no hunger while in the river some deep instinct to feed remains and is more likely to be awakened at this prime feeding time. The fish has being lying quietly all day, resting and with little action. The reduction in light may trigger restlessness and under the cloak of darkness the fish may feel safe to move into the shallows, to jump and to exercise. There is no way of knowing what the fish feel or think but the changes in behaviour are obvious. Through the night the movement of the clouds and the rising of the moon adjust and modify the level of darkness. Even a 'pitch black' night has some variations and although these are barely perceivable to us they may well affect the fish. There are nights when the fish that have seemed quiet and unmovable for hours will suddenly 'come on the take' only to switch off again after a short period of activity. Many times I have been fishing a pool with another with no results for some time and then suddenly both of us are into fish at the same time. Comparing notes with others who were fishing the river elsewhere on the same night have confirmed that the fish began to take during the same short period and there was no action before and after. This is undeniably a result of some very small change in conditions of light, temperature or pressure.

Dawson (West Country) advised giving up and going home if there are no takes in the first hour of darkness. Others recommend changing pools if similarly placed. Some recommended continuing with determination until dawn. Moving may be a good idea if the water has been disturbed but if the pool holds fish and the night is not too cold sooner or

later they will come on the take. The angler who continues through the night methodically and quietly through fish holding places will eventually take fish. I rarely have the stamina to continue much beyond midnight but when I have with dogged determination I have been rewarded. There are times when adapting tactics, changing flies, density of line or speed of retrieve may help but often it just necessary to keep going until the fish decide. Fishing is about patience if nothing else.

Often I have fished through to midnight without a touch and other fishermen have lost interest and gone home. Enjoying the night, the peace and quiet and the exercise of quiet rhythmic casting I have stayed on and before I too have lost enthusiasm I have had a fish on and then another. I wish I could identify the factors responsible. Some times there are obvious changes – a closing of the clouds or a freshening of the breeze - but more often than not I am unable to detect any at all.

Darkness inevitably brings a temperature drop and this will effect the oxygen levels in the river. As most of us will recall from our school science lessons cold water absorbs air more readily than hot water. The colder the water becomes – the more oxygen it contains and this must have some rejuvenation effect on the fish. Alas fish are cold-blooded creatures and as temperatures drop it is more difficult for them to use their muscles. In between there must be a balance where the water is sufficiently warm for the fish to move comfortably and 'breath' easily. The optimum seems to be around 13 – 15 degrees centigrade. Fortuitously this is a temperature that suits me as well. I can fish in comfort without too many restricting layers of clothing.

During the fishing season I watch the weather forecasts to check the wind direction and the cloud cover. I like a warm overcast night with a light breeze coming from the West to South

DATE	RIVER	BEAT	CONDITIONS
June 2003	Tavy	Middle	Low, clear water. Overcast sky 15C

NOTES
The weather forecast for this week predicted a warm night with cloud cover on Wednesday and so I pencilled in a night's fishing on this date. The forecast was correct and the air temperature on the bank was 15 C. Sport was fast and furious when the fish came on to the take one hour after dark. Lost three and landed two before midnight.

FISH CAUGHT	2 sea trout 3lb 7oz and 1lb 8 oz.	FLY/LURE	Size 8 Black fly

DATE	RIVER	BEAT	CONDITIONS
May 2003	Tavy	Middle	Low and clear river, overcast 10C

NOTES
A South East wind brought the first warmish night (10 C)that I could get to the river. I fished The Run with a sink tip line and a size 4 fly. At 10.30 a fish took and was netted. Some fifteen minutes later I had the gentlest of takes. When I tightened a heavy pull was returned and the pool exploded with spray as a heavy fish exploded on the surface and then was gone. I retrieved to find my flies still attached.

FISH CAUGHT	1 sea trout 3ln 5 oz	FLY/LURE	Size 4 Half Silver

DATE	RIVER	BEAT	CONDITIONS
June 1995	Tavy	Middle	River low and clear, No moon, cloud and very dark

NOTES
Hooked a large fish off the gravel bank opposite. It hit the fly as soon as it landed and cart wheeled all over the pool. Eventually it began to tire and I stepped forward and lowered the net into the water. I could not see the fish and was going much by feel and guesswork when I raised the net. The fish was not cleanly netted but the hook became caught on the mesh. At this point the fish regained its will to live and shook itself free. Had I been fishing with a single hook I think I would have landed my biggest sea trout to date.

FISH CAUGHT		FLY/LURE	Size 12 Treble – Black Special

East. When there is a northerly component to the wind it will be cold no matter how hot the day, especially if the sky is clear. Light rain does not have much effect and I have continued to fish with some success in prolonged drizzle. Heavy rain is a disaster however and brings leaves and debris to catch the line. There have been occasions when I have continued to fish at night in heavy rain out of stubbornness but with poor results.

I have experimented with all manner of lines and leaders over the years but now prefer to keep things simple. On warm nights (12 C+) I take a single rod set up with a floating line. On cool nights I may take two rods to the river. One is set up with a floating line and one with a sink tip. If nothing comes to the floating line during the first hour or two I will change rods. On my small rivers and relatively short pools a sink tip seems to suffice and a full 'sinker' that has to be rolled onto the surface to lift before back cast causes more disturbance than I am happy with. Over a season my approach brings me as many fish as I want and I have found a way of fishing that gives me immense enjoyment. If I became more efficient my personal limit might be arrived at much earlier

I begin the year fishing with flies tied on size 4 and 6 hooks but as the season progresses and the river shrinks I gradually reduce the size of flies I use until I am fishing size 10s and 12s in August. Invariably these are tied on single hooks and I experiment with patterns. I tie my own flies and am forever trying to create more effective variations.

On all but the brightest nights I fish with two flies - a point fly and a different pattern on a dropper, about 50cm up the cast. I use doubles, trebles and tubes during the day but find I get tangles far more easily at night and so I try keep things simple. Double or treble hooks will get caught in the net and are often time consuming to remove once a fish has been landed. There

have been many an occasion when I have missed netting a fish cleanly on the first lift but one point of the treble has become meshed. The hold on the net is always more secure than the hold on the fish and the result is an involuntary release! On moonlit nights with no cloud I sometimes fish without a dropper - employing one size 14 imitative pattern on a longer leader.

Finally when a fish is induced to take do you strike or not strike? It is surprising how hard a fish will pull at a fly or lure and not get hooked. I used to miss a lot of takes and thought I must be mistiming the strike to miss so many pulls. Advice from other anglers was contradictory and while most recommended waiting for the fish to hook itself these advocates I subsequently discovered do not land that many fish.

While my flies are sweeping through a pool it is usually impossible to see what is happening to them and I am operating entirely by feel. I hold my rod in my right hand and the line in my left feeling the flies move across the stream. I sense the changes in pressure as the current changes and respond by retrieving line or following the line with my rod. If I feel any halt in its progress or the pluck of a fish I respond immediately by raising the rod and tightening. This is not an aggressive strike but a positive tightening to feel for a fish.

On some nights several plucks at the fly can be felt as the cast swings through a pool. Some sea trout fishermen talk of the fish 'coming short'. They believe that sea trout are rising to touch or nip at the fly but shy away from a positive take – as they often behave to a spinner in the daytime. Special flies with flying treble hooks have been devised to counter this problem and I have met fishermen who cut the tails off their flies or tie them without tails in attempts to counter this perceived problem. But I am unconvinced by the theory. Those little plucks that are felt as the cast is fished I believe come

DATE	RIVER	BEAT	CONDITIONS
August 1996	Tavy	Lower	River low and clear, High cloud

NOTES

Fished down the run and had a savage take - the rod almost snatched from my hand. As I played it out it soon became clear that this was no giant fish. I netted and bagged a 1lb schoolie without getting out of the river.

Continuing down I had no more takes until the very end when after the slightest of taps the line went slack. I tightened and was immediately into a fish. Initially I thought it was another schoolie until it lept and proved to be a fish of a better size. This took a little more care to land. Keeping a tight line I reversed out of the water between the leaps it made. Eventually from the stability of the bank I could exert more control and after some excitement the best fish of the season was netted.

FISH CAUGHT	2 sea trout 1lb 2 ox and 5 lb 4 oz.	FLY/LURE	Size 10 Orange special

from small brown trout and par that attack a fly that very often is too big for them to swallow. Changing down to smaller patterns invariably results in the successful hooking of these small fish.

Actual sea trout takes come in many different ways and almost every one is different. Mostly it is the classic snatch as the fish seizes the fly and turns away. Sometimes there is a little tap as the fly is taken but if the fish continues to move forward the line may go slack. On other occasions the fly just seems to halt on its journey across the pool and you may think that you have caught the bottom. The fish

usually hooks itself with the typical snatch but if the line has any slack the fish will spit out the lure before the hook takes hold. It is therefore necessary to tighten when anything unusual is felt.

Once a fish is hooked I try to retain some pressure while I get loose line on the reel and gain some control. The fish will be allowed to run if it shows the determination and be guided up stream and away from the taking place if at all possible. This often creates some difficulty as sea trout are rarely cooperative and can leap and cavort all over a pool. When a fish leaps it is important not to allow it to get slack line and

to maintain contact with it. Bowing the rod to the fish is often recommended in other forms of fishing but will result in a lost fish when playing a sea trout. Early in the season I get over excited and apply too much pressure to hard fighting fish and get broken or the hook is pulled from the fresh fish's soft mouth. Keeping contact does not mean trying to haul the fish in before it is tired out.

Fish hooked in shallow water will show the greatest anxiety and will thrash on the surface as the rod point is held high. In such cases it is best to lower the rod tip to the water but point it away from the fish. This keeps a tight line and encourages the fish to begin swimming again. It will be less likely to throw the hook and the chances of landing it will increase significantly. Once its head is under the water the fish will tend to want to run upstream and into deeper sections where it can be tired with greater control before being led once more into the shallows to be netted.

Occasionally a fish will back away downstream and shake its head from side to side. These are usually the larger fish that have taken at the very tail of a pool. This happens more in the day time than at night but I land very few of these fish by day or in the dark. I tend to hang on in desperation and lose the fish as it assisted by pressure from the faster water. It happens very often with salmon in the daytime and I suspect that some of the fish I have lost while fishing in the dark have been the sea trout's larger cousin. I know I should remain calm, drop the rod and hope that with little pressure on the line the fish runs upstream and away from danger. But I always get excited and strategy gets forgotten.

Through the hours of darkness I try to fish with a sort of relaxed anticipation. For the most part I manage this until a big fish takes the fly.

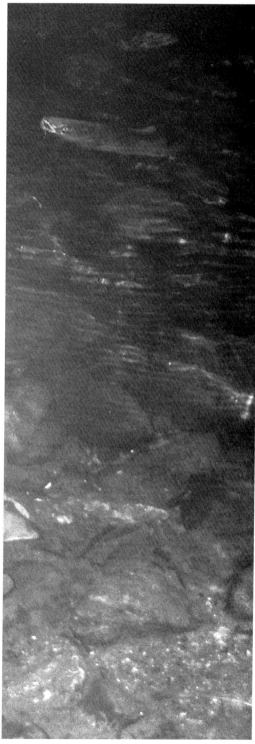

Chapter 6

The Line

Most fishermen I meet on the riverbank and engage in conversation want to talk about the fish and the fishing. They speak of fish taken, fish seen and fish lost. We discuss the river and related issues in the hope that we may gain information that could help secure a fish or two. Frustratingly I sometimes encounter one who insists on talking about his rod!

I include a chapter on kit with some reluctance. The equipment I use is not especially dear to me, what is much more important is how it is to be used. My apologies to the technophiles but for the most part I find that 'tackle talk' can be pretty tiresome. I know there are many who are of like mind but to be fair there is an enormous range of products now on the market and there are questions that are frequently asked. Perhaps some advice is appropriate, if just to help others evade the marketing traps.

Throughout these collected notes I have tried as far as possible to avoid mentioning any specific products or brands. There are occasions when I have found this difficult to avoid as the trade name is synonymous with the item talked about. The Mepps spoon in particular is an item that most fishermen are familiar and although there are other manufacturers making similar products, when I mention the 'Mepps' there cannot be confusion with non-revolving spoons or other forms of 'spinners'. Likewise the Rapala range of plugs were the first I discovered that were a good alternative to the Devon or Lane minnow. Although there are now many companies making similar lifelike plugs, most fellow anglers will know exactly what I am talking about when I speak of a 'Rapala'.

Where I use trade names it is in order to make it clear to the reader the type of tackle I am referring to and I wish to stress that it is not because I am recommending those specific brands. There seems to be a very wearisome trend prevalent in angling publications of giving brand names a high profile in fishing articles ('I took my X brand rod and Y brand reel and loaded it with Z brand line') Such statements immediately ring warning bells and suggest to me that the integrity of the information that follows may well be a little biased. Rarely do I bother to read any further.

Sadly, a frenzy of commercialism has swamped angling journalism and is distorting the perspective of those starting out on fishing. This is indicated by the marketing 'sound bites' being quoted on the riverbank. For a few anglers projecting the right image on the river is much more important than catching fish. They have to look the part, talk the talk and flaunt the right piscatorial bling. I have found that those who insist on talking about their tackle can not not be taken seriously and if they mention a 'designer' brand name you can safely disregard everything else they say. There is a very simple relationship between the amount spent on tackle and the number of fish caught. They are in inverse proportion and successful fishermen are invariably the ones who spend the least. The most successfull fishermen I have known (and most admired) over the years, have been mean old sods who wouldn't spend a penny more than necessary, and were proud of it!

Fishing has driven the development of many new and complex products and in the pursuit of that ever-elusive record breaker or just to catch one fish, all fishermen will yearn for the

DATE	RIVER	BEAT	CONDITIONS
July 2005	Tavy	Middle	Low clear 17C

NOTES

Tonight there were three of us on the pool, myself, old Roy and Rodney. Rodney wanted to talk a great deal. He distracted me. and although I tried to keep away from him he insisted on following me around. Perhaps he was afraid of the dark but he did not seem to want to know about the river or the fish, he insisted on talking about his new rod and hi tech reel. It had cost him, as he kept telling me, what for me would equate to a couple of months salary! He had memorised all the strap lines from the advertisements and quoted them endlessly. In the dark none of us could see it anyway. I was seriously unimpressed! All night he fussed and none of us caught anything until, thankfully, he left. The other rod then took three good fish and I managed a brace of schoolies.

We sat on the bench before we left for home to compare notes. Roy was a bit of a wag and in a good humour as he had outfished me, he kept quoting the new member and imitated his mannerisms. We sat on the pool and laughed and laughed - it was a good night after all. When I got home I wrote down something Roy had said. **" Brown trout give themselves up to those with skill and salmon to those with money but the sea trout is a very different creature - to catch sea trout you need soul!"**

FISH CAUGHT	2 sea trout both 1lb	FLY/LURE	Half Silver Size 10

DATE	RIVER	BEAT	CONDITIONS
1995 July	Tavy	Lower	Low and clear – new moon

NOTES

I met one of the more senior members on the river at dusk. He was dressed in a tweed jacket and hat and with a split cane rod and wicker creel looked like a ghost from the past In the growing darkness with the last light of the sunset the world was sepia and I felt I had stepped into an Edwardian photograph. I engaged him in conversation and we talked of conservation and traditional values which he seemed to epitomise. He subsequently hooked, landed and returned about 15 sea trout to my one. Even when encouraged to take over his stand and cast to his direction my carbon fibre rod and poly coated line could not match the casts of his split cane and silk. (I also failed to equal his water craft.)

FISH CAUGHT	1 sea trout 1lb 4 oz.	FLY/LURE	Mallard and silver LS 10

DATE	RIVER	BEAT	CONDITIONS
August 1992	Walkham	Upper	Some rain muddied the river slightly but no rise

NOTES

We had the first rain for some weeks and I hurried to have a look at the upper Walkham. I took my light split cane spinning rod and a tin of Mepps. Alas there were no sea trout to be found.

Arrived home to find my split can rod had broken in the boot of the car. My Wellingtons must have bounced onto it as I drove along the track!. Is it repairable?

FISH CAUGHT	A dozen or so small browns - all returned with no damage.	FLY/LURE	Size 2 Mepps

piece of kit that may just make the difference. The tackle industry is enormous – it sponsors a great deal of research and is quick to adapt materials created by aerospace industries. There are many wonderful products out there but we need to temper our enthusiasm for shopping and keep our focus on fishing. We should recall that man has been catching fish long before the arrival of high tech products. Success was possible without modern materials because we learnt to understand fish and their environment. No amount of cash will compensate for skills and knowledge that has been long lost. I commend fishermen to spend time regaining this knowledge before spending money on uneccessary and expensive equipment.

There are clearly many for whom owning exclusive tackle is important and if it makes them happy I should be happy, but in fact, I am a little sad. My tackle is for fishing – not for status and as I am somewhat embarrassed by 'designer labels', the only 'posh' kit I own (bought second hand) has had the decals rubbed off.

The most important piece of kit for any fly fisher is the fly line. It took me many years to discover this but a good line will cast well on almost any rod while poor lines are difficult to cast on the best rods. Fortunately there is a good range of lines on the market, at almost reasonable prices, and they will all perform very well. Probably because a line has limited sex appeal it has proved difficult to project as a 'must have' by the marketing people. Subsequently fly lines are not subjected to the same extremes of prices as rods and reels.

Many modern fly lines are designed for the reservoir fly fisherman and are capable of reaching great distances. I have little need for range but do need a fly line that shoots through the rings with ease. Especially when I am trying to flick and roll a fly out onto the water from amongst trees and bushes. I have tried 'budget

lines' and 'mill ends' and found them adequate but there are times when I need something a little more slippery. This is one area where I no longer compromise and all of my current fly lines cost me more than the rods I use them on.

Most of my night fishing is done with a 'weight forward #6 or #7' floating line. One that is white in colour. The colour enables me to see where the line is on lighter nights and helps me maintain some control. A WF #7 handles a good range of flies and lures with relative sensitivity and allows me to reach all the corners of my favourite pools with ease. The WF#6 allows me to drop small flies with minimum disturbance on still and brighter nights. Early in the season and on colder nights I may use a sink tip line. This enables me to fish my heavier flies with a little more comfort and try to get them down amongst the fish who are reluctant to rise far off the bottom. I would like a line with a white main section and a neutral coloured sinking section but have yet to find one. I have experimented with a line with a clear intermediate tip and a white 'glow in the dark' shooting section and I may be using this more often.

During the day and in low water I often use the same rods that are used at night. The WF#6 is excellent for upstream nymphing between the boulder strewn runs but when the river is high and the water heavy I use a 'WF #8' sink tip line on a longer rod. The line I have is light green with a darker sinking section. The line enables me to fish a greater range of flies including weighted trebles and tubes. I find that full sinking lines are harder to cast without causing some disturbance to the water surface. I know they have their devotees but on my rivers and for much of my fishing I am not using a great length of line. With less than twenty metres of line in use the sink tip line gets the lure down almost as far as a full sinker and is much easier to handle. I am sure that if I persevered with full sinking lines I could catch a few more

fish, especially on colder nights but it is not a method I particularly enjoy.

I do try to look after my fly lines and after every couple of outings they get a little care and attention. I stretch them out in a zigzag across my garden and tension them lightly. Once stretched, the lines get cleaned with mild soap and water and polished with a proprietary line treatment. (I have found that liquid car wax is as good.) The light stretching helps remove any kinks or coils and the polishing helps ensure the line shoots through the rings. If you feel that your old line is getting tired and needs replacing try giving it this treatment before ditching it.

Fishing rods are now constructed in 'high tech' factories with amazingly fine tolerances and quality control. The quality of the construction varies, but not so much that someone of my casting ability would really worry about. I rarely need to make a long cast and so I do not need the range that some still water or big-river fly fishers demand. I am rarely using the tiny flies used on chalk streams and do not require that degree of delicacy. I use a range of wet flies and lures of varying weights and I need to be able to place each fly on a dustbin lid within the ranges of five to twenty yards. Usually I will be struggling with limited space for back casting. I am often flicking, side casting, catapult and roll casting, usually in complete darkness and could well be hanging off a holly tree and casting with one hand. Most of today's 'budget' rods will be capable of meeting this level of performance and more. In fact, at country show casting displays, I have seen an 'expert' demonstrate casts equal in distance and accuracy to that which I need, with a broomstick!

There are those of my acquaintance who prefer to use traditional equipment. They feel that this is not only an important aspect of the culture but also is more sporting. I have every respect for this approach and miss meeting a lovely man who used to turn up in a Norfolk jacket and a deerstalker, armed with a beautiful split cane rod and sensible sized, bent wood net that he made himself.

For me, and my style of fishing, the traditional cane rod requires too much care and attention and they can be horrendously expensive to repair. I have a couple of cane rods in the cupboard but do not use them regularly. I am very tough on my kit. My fishing takes me to wild places where apart from some occasional cautious pruning they are not ordered by man. They are difficult places in which to travel on foot, especially in the dark and trying to avoid the use of a torch. I fall over, I break rods and would be distraught if I snapped an heirloom.

I tend to buy second hand or 'sale' rods. I have no concern for make or label but when it looks like the very thing I need to present lighter, heavier, bigger or smaller flies and reach that special, difficult lie, I am sometimes tempted. I have far too much kit and nearly all of my fishing is carried out with the fly rod I first bought – the others rarely come out of the cupboard.

In about 1980 I bought a second hand 8' 6" # 6/7 carbon fly rod for £10. It has served me extremely well and is amazingly versatile; what is more surprising is, considering the treatment it has had, that I have not broken it. The little rod has landed me tiny brown trout from the Dartmoor streams, my largest chalk stream brown, over-fattened still water rainbows, my biggest Tavy salmon (12.5 lb) and even bass from the North Devon beaches. It comes into its own during the main summer run of sea trout when it will allow me to fish a pair of small flies in confined spaces with more accuracy than I really need. With space to back cast it will put out a good 20+ metres of line but more importantly it will flick out 10 metres from tight corners. I take this to the river with reel loaded with a WF#7 floater on dark nights and a WF#6 on the lighter nights.

es under different conditions, with, I am sure, beneficial
sults.

In the past few years increased interest has been dis-
...ayed in the relative merits of flies of different types for
...ght fishing... a series of articles and lett... on the
...atter appeared in the ... the en...
...1944, and continued through 1945 an... to 1946
...hese dealt with questions of light absorp...n, reflected
...ght, translucency, fluorescence, vibration, and kindred
...ubjects. While som... of these ...ulations were of a
...omewhat scienti... ...ertheless opened u...
...ost interest... ...tion evoked...
...ore compreh... ...gent discussion than an...
...at had appeared in the angling press for years. I wa...
...rprised at the number of contributors who had so muc...
...f interest to... ...e obvious...
...ery keen and extensive... ...he amount o...
...hought that had been given to the subject, and the exten...
...o which experiment had been carried by some.

...Mr. Eggington, who started the ball rolling, claims tha...

...matter appeared in the *Fishing Gazette* towards th...
...f 1944, and continued through 1945 and into...
These dealt with questions of light absorption, ref...
...ight, translucency, fluoresc... ...ration, and ki...
...ubjects. While som... of these ...tributions were...
...omewhat scientific m... they nevertheless opene...
...ost interest... ...stas ... the wh... ...uestion evol...
...ore compr... ...e m... intell... ...discussion than...
...hat had app... ...g the... ...ngl... press for years. ...
...urprised at the num... of contributors who had so...
...f interest to say... ...the subject, and at the obvi...
...ery keen and ...tensive... ...played, ...he amou...
...hought that h... ...een g... ...n to the... ...ect, and the e...
...o which experi...ent h... been ca... ...some.

Mr. Eggington, who started the ball rolling, claims
...he best fly for night ...shing must be a white one o...
...ushy type with silver ...el ribbing, contending that...
...fly transmits all light th...re may be, while the tinsel...
...eflect direct moon rays on a clear moonlight night.

DATE	RIVER	BEAT	CONDITIONS
August 1989	Plym	Shaugh	Low and clear

NOTES

Arrived at the river to find Gareth on the river bank and having not seen him for a while I struck up a conversation to catch up. He was not a happy man and I discovered that the previous night he had brought two brand new rods and had laid one down on the track while tackling up. A mountain cyclist had come down the path out of the dark – run over his new rod and with a cheery greeting, disappeared again into the night!
I must be more careful where I put my rods in the dark!

FISH CAUGHT	1 sea trout 1lb 4oz	FLY/LURE	Black Pennel 10

DATE	RIVER	BEAT	CONDITIONS
June 2006	Tavy	Lower	Low and clear

NOTES

Driving down to the river I found a stranger manoeuvring in the parking space. Thinking he was about to leave and was creating space for me I began to pull into the space by the side. "Stop", was shouted but at the same time as a sharp crack. I had run over a rod left on the ground!

FISH CAUGHT	2 Sea trout 2lb and 2lb 2oz	FLY/LURE	Special size 8

DATE	RIVER	BEAT	CONDITIONS
July 2005	Tavy	Middle	Low clear river. Thin cloud, full moon low in the sky. 18C dropping to 15C

NOTES

A very light night. Although the moon is very low in the sky and not shining directly on the river it was very bright. Many fish were moving and with the good visibility I could see my cast landing gently. The new 'budget rod' was able to cast 20 metres of WF6 line with little effort and drop my flies with no disturbance.
The fish came on after Midnight, when it noticeably cooled and I took and subsequently landed 5 fish - losing another 2 before 1.00am (3 on the dropper). All fish came when casting a longish line (15metres) downstream under bushes. The cheap rod handled the largest fish with no difficulty and I felt confident it could handle anything the river could throw at me!
Roy was also fishing but with a heavier line and he took his first fish as I was leaving at 1.30am. I caught up with him later and discovered that he also finished with a good bag but he had to work hard for it. The lighter rod was the better tool - even if it was a cheap one!

FISH CAUGHT	5 sea trout 12 oz – 2lb4oz (2 returned)	FLY/LURE	2 – size 10 LS half silver (+1 lost) 3 – size 10 special

I have a heavier 9'6" #7/8 carbon rod that I use early in the season when I want to fish a larger – perhaps weighted fly at night or during heavy water through summer spates. It was produced and marketed as a 'still water lure' rod and is more than adequate for the purpose to which I put it. Again this was bought second hand for a small proportion of its original cost and has handled sea trout to 6 lb and several grilse of up to 7lb with ease. It is too long to use under the canopies of oak where much of my fishing takes place but is useful on one beat where I need the height to back cast over an overgrown hedge.

A few seasons ago I bought a 9'0" 6/7 rod to complement my 8'6" rod when night fishing. For a few seasons – especially on cooler nights I took two rods to the river, one with a floating line and one with a sink tip. Both had been set up in my garage before leaving home and this saved me the trouble of changing reels and threading lines in the dark. It proved a useful experiment and occasionally I still take the two rods when undecided on tactics, but I am not sure it helps me to catch any more fish. I much prefer to be unencumbered by an extra rod. It has to be left somewhere while fishing and it is very easy to get it broken in the dark.

In 2005 I bought a 'brand' new 9' - 4 piece #5/6 carbon rod for £16 - just a few pounds more than the second hand rod bought in 1980. Twenty-five years on and for what in real terms is a great deal less money I have bought a rod that looks a lot better made. It was bought with a fishing trip in mind - I did not want to worry about losing an old favourite. The new rod has now had a full season's use and I have not been able to fault its performance. The gap in price between this budget model and the equivalent made by a 'designer' label can approach a thousand pounds. The difference in quality is minimal and I find it hard to justify paying such a 'mark up' just for a name.

For leaders I currently favour fluorocarbon line as this sinks easily and does not create surface 'wake'. Fluorocarbon tippets have allowed me to dispense with the braided leader previously used for night fishing and I no longer need to stop to degrease the tippet every half hour or so. I had preferred the tapered braided leaders as they help ensure a good turn over but they seem to create a little splash upon hitting the water. On windless night this can create a commotion that is best avoided. It can be disastrous on moonlit nights and so I now create a short loop from clear braided backing and attach my fluorocarbon to this with a loop knot. The fluorocarbon leader is constructed of three sections tapering from 14lb to 10lb to 6 or 8lb at night and possible 4lb by day if the water is low. The sections are joined with a four-turn water knot and I usually employ one dropper about half a metre from the point fly.

Lines and leaders obviously need to be held on a reel and I have a number of different makes and models that have almost all been obtained second hand. Again I spurn 'designer labels' and look for something entirely functional that is going to take a lot of rough treatment. I have yet to wear out or break a fly reel. For most of my night fishing I use a pair of automatic (clockwork) models. I believe these are no longer manufactured. They fell out of fashion as the spring makes them very heavy and casting with the pendulum effect requires some practice. The delight is that when a fish is hooked, one pull on the little lever/trigger and all the loose line is immediately drawn onto the reel. I can focus on the fish without falling over or stepping on the hanging loops. I then play the fish 'off the reel' – the tension of the clockwork spring is just right for maintaining contact without risking being broken off. I can concentrate on maintaining contact and steering the fish where I need it to go. In total darkness with a lively fish this is a significant bonus.

DATE	RIVER	BEAT	CONDITIONS
June 1989	Plym	Shaugh	River had risen a little and was carrying peat stain and sediment

NOTES

I took a good sea trout at my feet in the Scout Hut Pool to a size 2 Mepp. In Beech Tree Pool I had a powerful take in the middle while I was fishing from the neck. Not quite a double figure fish but the largest hooked to date cavorted all over the pool splashing and leaping. As it began to tire I worked around the tree to the tail and looked for a place to beach it. I had hoped to guide it into the small ribbon stream where I could slide it onto the bank as I had done before. But that was now full with spate water. The fish was quiet and could be netted but I had no net. In attempting to guide it into a shallow bay it flipped over and was lost.

FISH CAUGHT	I sea trout 2lb 2oz	FLY/LURE	Size 2 Mepp

DATE	RIVER	BEAT	CONDITIONS
September 2005	Tavy	Middle Beat	River had risen a little and was carrying peat stain.

NOTES

I was unaware that my net had collected a short piece of bramble that had knitted the mesh together. Before long I had cause to put it to use when a lively salmon took at the end of Lower Dukes pool. When I attempted to scoop it up, the net failed to open and the fish was balanced bouncing on the flat disk of tight and tangled net. The hook caught in the mesh and I had to use the net like a racket to bat the fish onto the bank. The salmon immediately threw the hook and I dropped upon it but it slipped between my knees and launched itself back into the river.

FISH CAUGHT	I salmon lost about 7lb.	FLY/LURE	I" Blue Tube

DATE	RIVER	BEAT	CONDITIONS
August 2003	Tavy	Lower Beat	Low, clear, overcast no moon. 15C

NOTES

Just as I was starting I took a good sea trout while wading in The Run but the dropper became caught in the net. I had to return to the shore to remove it and then found I had left my torch behind. The hook was stuck hard and in the end I decided to walk back to the car and sort it out using the interior light. This worked but upset my night sight and finding my way back to the river was difficult. Eventually I acclimatised and began fishing again but I lost my rhythm and cast a tight loop that caught back on itself. This created another tangle and I had to make the trek once more to the car. This time I decided to give up and have an early night. A lack of preparation had lost me what may have been the best night of the season.

FISH CAUGHT	I sea trout 1lb 10oz.	FLY/LURE	Size 10 Special.

Unfortunately the automatic reels I have, will not take a line larger than WF#7 and then only with limited backing. I have to resort to traditional style reels for heavier lines or where I may need more backing. In a tackle shop sale I recently purchased a 'large arbor' reel with spare spool for the heavier lines I sometimes use for spring sea trout and autumn salmon.

I also have two spinning rods but they see less work these days. I have a 7' 6" - 7 – 20gm carbon rod that allows me to flick a small lure up under the bushes. This is used with a small fixed spool reel and 8lb monofilament line. To the 8lb mainline I attach a metre of 15lb fluorocarbon to take any abrasion from rocks and foliage. When I used a Mepps type - revolving spoon I tied on a small swivel to the main line and attached about half a metre of clear mono between it and the spoon but I have not spun for sea trout using this type of tackle for many years. I prefer to use a Rapala type of plug if fly-fishing is not an option. When using plugs I do not use any swivel and attach the plug directly with a loop knot. The small plug is an excellent alternative to rotating minnows. Whilst wobbling enticingly they do not revolve and therefore do not add excessive twist to the line.

My other spinning rod is a 8'6" 15 – 30 gm 2 piece that I made myself from a plain blank. I use it with a multiplier occasionally for autumn salmon but these days it is used more for free lining sand eels in Plymouth Sound with bass in mind. On the multiplier I have modern braided line of about 20lb test. This is a yellow coloured line as it helps me see where the lure is fishing. Again a metre or so of clear monofilament is attached to the line via a small swivel.

For many years I did not carry a net – it seemed a bit presumptuous and I liked to travel light. I preferred to beach my fish or hand them out. Then one day on the Plym I lost a (possibly) double figure fish that I might have secured had

I a net. I went out and bought one the following day and have carried a net on most occasions since.

Beaching a fish is often the easiest way of landing it but it is almost certain to injure the fish as it thrashes on the pebbles. I sometimes still use this method if in a convenient position and the fish is definitely going to be kept 'for the pot'. Handing a fish out is more humane and I practise this with small browns inadvertently hooked. Sea trout however are prone to finding a second wind once in the hand and on more than one occasion a fish I thought was beaten and have lifted has leapt from my hand and with slack line has thrown the hook. Sea trout are now nearly always netted.

Folding landing nets have served me well over the years. I currently have a large triangular net with a telescopic handle that has been able to scoop up every sea trout and almost all the salmon I have caught. The spring steel belt clip on my latest model has broken and so when fishing I unfold it and slot the handle between the double section of my bag strap and it sits comfortably at my back. I have since discovered a 'gye style' net that has a harness/strap with a 'velcro' quick release. This has completed one season successfully and for the time being has replaced the folding version.

I sometimes feel somewhat vertically challenged and the nets I have tend to droop and get tangled in brambles and collect dead sticks. This can cause the net to bind together and I have lost fish as a result. To overcome this I bunch the net together and fasten it with a thin elastic band. When netting a fish the band pulls away or breaks.

I have mentioned that I take a bag. Again this was a luxury I denied myself for many years, as again it seemed to presume I was going to catch something! It was not that I was superstitious its just it seemed a bit audacious. Eventually I

DATE	RIVER	BEAT	CONDITIONS
July 2005	Tavy	Middle	River Low and clear. No cloud -WNW 15 C

NOTES
Arrived at the river to find another angler's car but could find no one at the main pools – he had evidently gone downstream. When it became dark I started and standing well back from the edge and casting out just a yard or so I immediately had a take and landed a schoolie. A few more casts and I was into a better fish. It was going to be a good night!? Unfortunately the dropper became enmeshed in the net and I lost the fish. While trying to untangle the cast by feel I was distracted and frustrated by fish leaping all over the pool and just then the other angler appeared with a powerful head light. He tried to help me by putting his light on my net and it unfortunately lit up the entire bank. I decided to retire to retie my cast. While I did this I suggested Flasher take up my (successful) stand. Once reorganised I moved around the corner to a usually less productive spot but one that may not have been affected by the torch. We both fished until 1.00 am. I had one more fish but he left without moving a single sea trout. I am not sure if it was any undetectable change in the presure or temperature or the torch that had put the remaining fish off – I suspect the torch.

FISH CAUGHT	2 seat trout 1lb, 1 sea trout 2lb	FLY/LURE	Size 10 special.

DATE	RIVER	BEAT	CONDITIONS
August 2003	Tavy	Middle Beat	Low clear, waning moon

NOTES
Took 2 sea trout in the Run on and was returning to the main pool to see how the other rods had progressed. The Surgeon had just hooked and landed his first sea trout of the night and as I stepped forward to congratulate him I felt his rod under my foot. Fortunately I realised before I put any pressure on it and was able to bend and pick it up undamaged. But it was a close thing. There were two of us around him with his very black rod on the ground in the dark. Must watch this in future. I took some comfort in the light reflective strips on my rods that do provide some extra warning.

FISH CAUGHT	2 sea trout both 10 oz	FLY/LURE	Size 10 Special.

DATE	RIVER	BEAT	CONDITIONS
June 1994	Walkham	Upper	Low, clear some moon

NOTES
I had agreed to take a friend's visitor sea trout fishing. He was, it was claimed a very keen angler but had never caught a sea trout. I arrived to collect the 'fisherman' to find the party still at dinner and was ushered in to join them for coffee while they finished desert. My heart sank when entering the room I found Eric sat at the table and eating his pudding in a fishing waistcoat - one overstocked with badges and bling.! This did not bode well and the night was spent in boastful prattle until dinner and wine caught up with him and he wanted to get to bed.

FISH CAUGHT	0	FLY/LURE	

gave in and used a succession of Government surplus kit bags until my wife felt sorry for me and bought a smart waxed cotton and leather trimmed bag with a detachable liner. At first I thought it was a little 'flash' for me but it has proved long lasting and very useful. It enables me to carry all manner of small items when not wearing a jacket and have limited pockets. The waterproof liner makes it easy to carry and deal with fish. On arriving home late at night the liner is taken from the bag, folded with the fish inside and eased into the fridge. I then go to bed and clean the fish in the morning.

A torch is obviously a useful item to take to the water when night fishing. It would seem a necessity but on the many occasions that I have forgotten a torch or the battery has run out I have been able to operate with some success. For most of the time I try to avoid using a light anyway but find it helpful (almost essential) when I need to select and tie on a new fly.

When I remember! I take two lights to the river. This first is a small waterproof hand torch that I keep in my pocket or bag. This is for finding my way back after fishing or for any emergencies. The second is a small medical light that was supplied with a headband. I have dispensed with the headband preferring to carry it in my pocket and clip the light onto my lapel or bag strap when needed. The problem with a 'head lamp' is that the beam can swing all over the place as you move around and flash in places you would rather it didn't. Clipped onto my chest the small torch gives sufficient light to tie knots and check flies as I kneel down in the bushes with my back to the water. This effectively minimises any disturbance. I also stick a small strip of white reflective tape to my rods, to the handles of my nets and the inside of the flap of my bag. These help a great deal if I put an item down in the dark and I am trying to find it again. Carbon rods are often black and both my nets have been likewise manufactured, in Model T colours. The reflective strip is

attached to the rod behind the reel seat so that it is facing away from the river while fishing. The tape on the net is wound around the handle and can be seen from 360 degrees but as this is attached to my back while fishing it is unlikely to worry the fish. A small square is stuck on the end of the long handle and this helps me judge the position of the net and ensure it is the right way up when netting a fish in the dark.

There have been occasions when I have put down my net after landing a fish and resumed fishing only to find I have wandered away from the location and cannot find the net in the dark. Flashing around with a torch would be not be sensible or politic and on occasions I have been reduced to feeling my way up and down the bank in order to relocate a lost net. Reflective tape helps avoid some of the tactile delights waiting on the riverbank! If I put my bag down anywhere I leave the flap open to that the reflective tape will guide me back to it.

It is not a good idea to lay rods down on the ground at any time but especially not when retying flies or untying knots in the dark. It is easy to become sufficiently disorientated that a step to one side causes you to step on the rod. When fishing with others who may rush up to see your catch or step forward to see what fly you are tying on, a rod on the ground quickly becomes a broken rod.

In my pockets I carry a small pair of scissors and a pair of forceps. My dentist does not recommend biting through monofilament and forceps are often the only way of retrieving a fly from the back of a sea trout's mouth. I also carry a hook sharpener. When fishing slowly around the rocks and ledges I often get caught up on the bottom and this blunts the point of the hook. When I manage to free a line that has been snagged I feel the hook points with the tips of my fingers and if they have been blunted I re-sharpen them by feel, with this small tool. This avoids changing flies that may be otherwise

DATE	RIVER	BEAT	CONDITIONS
August 1994	Walkham	Magpie	Low/clear

NOTES
I was directed to collect some shopping on my way to the river. In the supermarket I felt a bit self conscious in my old fishing cords and jumper but here leaning over the frozen food chest I came face to face with another fisherman! The chap was fitted out from the 'Look like a Real Fisherman' catalogue with fly covered hat, camouflaged shirt and waistcoat bedecked with every possible item of tackle dangling and jangling including one of those natty but useless little bent wood nets.
People were staring and I became terrified that others might think we were 'together'. I complete my erand and left with some haste. On the way out I thought that perhaps I was a little unkind and he was probably going to a fancy dress party.

FISH CAUGHT	2 browns - returned	FLY/LURE	Mallard and silver 10

DATE	RIVER	BEAT	CONDITIONS
November 2000	Plym	Shaugh	River up after overnight rain beginning to clear

NOTES
A tree had fallen below the bridge creating a barrier to running salmon. I found a pool with half a dozen salmon in below the obstacle. In the clearing water they could be seen in a neat line in the deepest run.

A large Mepp was taken second cast and the fish obliged me by fighting it out in the small pool. When it began to tire I tried to tail it but it toppled over the lip of the pool and into the run. I tried to keep up with the fish that headed seaward with my lure. The river runs through a small holly filled gorge at this point and I had to shoulder my way through the prickles and over the rocks. At one stage I had to hold the rod in my teeth as I used both arms to get along a high bank. The fish was lost in the Style Pool.

I returned to the pool via the path and immediately hooked another salmon. This one took off downstream immediately and again I fought my way over the rocks and through the thorns. When I reached the point where I had to hold the rod in my teeth I gave the fish line and it came unstuck. A sucker for punishment

I returned to the hot spot and within a couple of casts had a third fish on. This did not delay but headed downstream and again I followed now knowing every, handhold, foothold and whipping holly branch but to no avail. This fish was also lost in the Style Pool that was like a boiling cauldron in the spate.

By now I had had enough – my trousers were torn, my knee was bleeding and my hands and face scratched and raw. Thankfully my waxed jacket had protected me from the worst of the barbed brush.

On the way home I had a couple of last casts in the Scout Hut Pool and hooked a fourth salmon. This kindly stayed in the pool and was beached successfully on the grass. |

FISH CAUGHT	1 salmon 8lb (3 lost)	FLY/LURE	Mepp Size 4 gold

working well. Together with a spool or two of monofilament and a couple of fly boxes this is all I feel I need.

I wear glasses for reading and close work and need these to retie lines. My distance vision is fine and I can fish without glasses. In fact at night I find I can see better without them but usually keep them on for eye protection. I have never hit my face with a mistimed lift into a cast but it could easily happen. During the day I wear Polaroid bifocal sunglasses as these help me see beyond the reflections on the water and retie my line.

If I am intending to wade a great deal I wear a 'life preserver' of the automatic inflation type. My 'exploding braces' have never been put to use but are there should I need them. I really should wear them for all of my fishing and I applaud those who diligently play safe!

There remains the other matter of dress! I am not particularly worried about what I look like when on the river but try to dress appropriate to the occasion. When fishing, function overrides everything. I need to feel unencumbered but warm and dry. There is a vast range of clothing designed for the walker that is eminently suitable with modern fabrics that wick away moisture, breathe and conserve heat. These are excellent but I find myself favouring traditional materials for most of my fishing.

I usually wear a lightweight waxed cotton jacket. This is now nearly twenty years old and has been back to the manufacturers twice for refurbishment but will see many more years yet. (I hope). The traditional waxed jacket has many drawbacks. It is not a warm fabric and in cold weather it becomes very stiff. Although it sheds water very well, in prolonged downpours eventually it is penetrated and it becomes quite heavy. Its advantages include the fact that it is practically indestructible and for the fisherman

who has to fight bramble and thorn it provides a level of protection that is unrivalled. There are times when I need to slide down a bank to net a fish or push my way through scrub to get to cast to a little-known lie. I rarely fish in continuing rain and it provides more than adequate protection from showers and splashes.

I try to be as unobtrusive as possible when on the river. Not only do I not want to be seen by the fish but also I enjoy the opportunities to enjoy close encounters with other wild life. My fishing clothing is in olive, green or a neutral colour but I think that military style camouflage clothing is unnecessary. It seems to smack of overkill. I feel no need to advertise the fact that I am a fisherman and I have found that the excess of pockets clips and rings that plague garments designed for fishing provide ideal places for hooks and lines to catch and snag. They are just for decoration that I have no need of.

Unless I forget and leave it behind I wear a hat when fishing. This is for entirely functional reasons I feel a bit stupid but my hair has thinned on top and I find I get sunburnt in the summer or cold during the winter. A brimmed hat helps the eyes adjust to peering into dark water and is essential during daytime fishing. At night, a brim helps protect the back of the head and the ears from mistimed casts. It also shields my eyes from the stars, which on bright nights affect my night vision.

I have experimented with tweed caps, baseball caps and all manner of 'flower-pots'. Tweeds can get a little hot and baseball caps, while shielding the face effectively leaves the ears exposed. They also make you look a little like an adolescent trying to hide his acne. My favourite is a light olive cotton bush hat that I borrowed from my father. It is light and comfortable in the sunshine and wide enough to stop my ears from getting pierced by wayward hooks. Dad no longer needs it and it has memories.

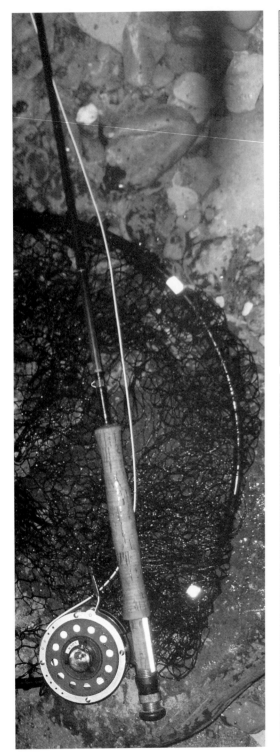

DATE	RIVER	BEAT	CONDITIONS
July 2005	Tavy	Lower	Low clear – new moon below horizon 17C

NOTES

I fished down the Run and while I had more action than anticipated I only succeeded in landing two fish. Peal continued to show and I was certain that a significant shoal had taken up residence. I stopped to rest the fish and while exchanging notes with the other rods I discovered that they were fishless and, had not enjoyed a fruitful season.

While I was very tempted to commiserate and then go and fish over the shoal again I felt I should share my luck and I suggested that one or the other fish the hot spots instead. One agreed and I suggested where he should enter the water, wade and cast. After half an hour of casting over a taking shoal he had not a touch. I could not understand this as he was fishing well - dropping his line delicately and was not splashing around in the river. What was going wrong?

When I walked down the bank see how the other rod had fared I could see the angler standing in the middle of the river. It was now as dark as it was going to get but his light colour 'designer' fishing shirt seemed to glow in dark and I could see him from over fifty yards away. Was this the problem?

FISH CAUGHT	2 sea trout 2lb 2oz and 1 lb	FLY/LURE	Size 10 Half silver

My feet are essential parts of my body that I want to have long use of. I try to look after them. I hate having wet feet and so try to keep them warm and dry when fishing. So I wear waterproof boots when on the river. I have three different types but most of the time I find myself wearing thigh waders. Although I try keep out of the water as much as possible eventually I have to enter the river to net a fish, to cast to an otherwise unreachable lie or wade the stream to retrieve a snagged lure. They also protect my legs from splashes and the rain or dew that clings to summer-high grass and ferns.

I have tried all sorts of waders over the years and some have barely lasted a season before they have had to be thrown out. The longest serving pair is made of neoprene and have ordinary cleated soles. These are still in use after at least six years. The longevity of these waders has surprised me and although they have been pierced and torn many times, they are easily glued back together. Also if standing in water for any length of time they do insulate me from the cold.

I also possess a pair of breathable chest waders. They were bought to fish one particular beat where it proved a little deep for thigh waders. The 'chesties' have excellent spiked soles that give good grip on slimy pebbles. They are light and comfortable to wear on the bank but standing for any time in cold water becomes uncomfortable. Probably thick socks and thermal underwear are needed but this would defeat the objective of a lightweight garment. I have been tempted to change to neoprene but chest waders in this material make middle-aged men with any (beer?) belly look a little comical.

Fortunately much of my fishing is carried out from the bank and a pair of Wellington boots often meets my needs. When it has been dry and my legs are not likely to be soaked by dew or rain drops on high grass or bracken wellingtons will be my first choice. Even on the driest days there are boggy, wet and muddy patches by the river and I may need to paddle a little to net a fish. Shoes are never an option. Trainers would be destroyed very quickly but wellies are cheap and hard-wearing. They can often be patched and glued to extend their lifespan and my last pair survived all manner of abuse for at least ten years.

I must admit that using appropriate kit can make fishing more enjoyable but I must stress that it has to be kept in proportion. I am happy to pay out for my licence and permits but spending an excess on tackle seems to me to close the gap between catching a fish and buying a fish. The real rewards are to be found in taking a difficult fish by using more competence than cash. I have noted that the most successful fishermen always seem to use the most modest tackle. Having equipped themselves sparingly they have focussed on learning about the river and its ways. Clearly they have been all the more richer for it.

Those who look down their noses at budget tackle have no place on the sea trout river and thankfully, in the main they stay away. The snobbery that has afflicted other branches of fishing inhibit beginners and scare off the youngsters.

As we waited for darkness by the river one night, old Roy rightly pointed out that before the arrival of carbon, kevlar, gortex and fluorocarbon, past club members were each regularly taking up to 250 sea trout a year from the pool we were soon to fish. Their cane or greenheart rods and gut casts were primitive by our standards but they had a sophisticated understanding of the river, if a somewhat cavalier attitude to conservation!

The fish are still there and the secrets still lie in stealth, skill and study. Over-engineered tackle creates no advantage what-so-ever.

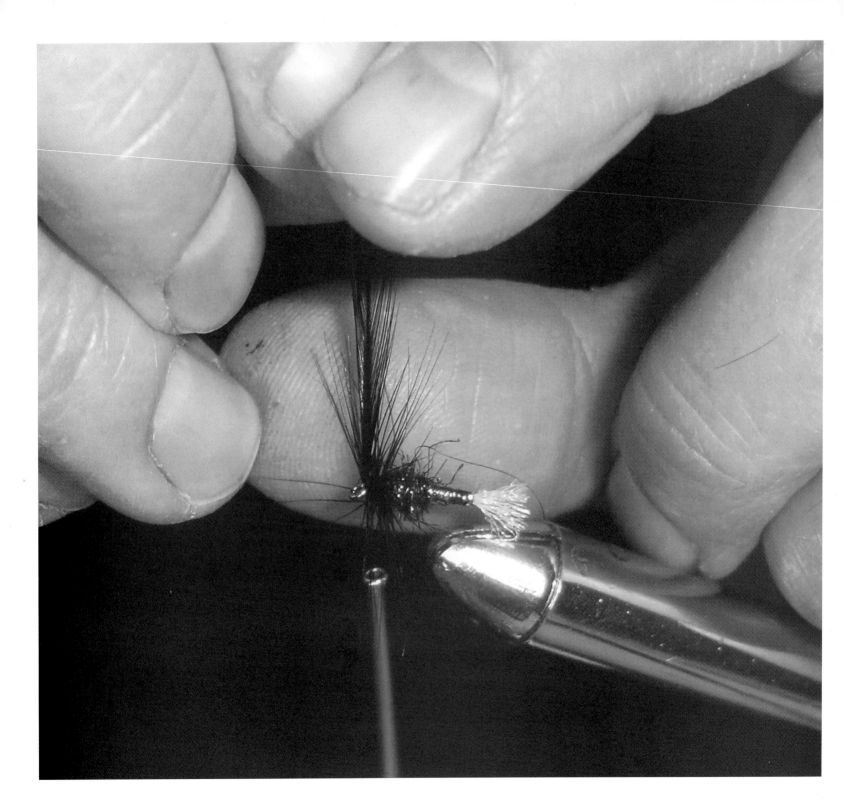

Chapter 7

The Vice

I once asked a veteran sea trout angler to recommend patterns to use when sea trout fishing and he replied 'fish something that you are confident with'. This disappointed me at the time, and I felt it was nonsense. For if I then had any confidence in any particular fly I would not be asking for advice. But I think I now know what he was trying to say - it is important to have some belief that the fly could deceive or lure a fish as fishing with confidence usually results in fishing with success. Perhaps he should have picked a standard pattern and offered it with enthusiasm - I may have used it with conviction and achieved more success.

I find that when my confidence is high and I am fishing over lies with keen anticipation, I do seem to get more takes. There is no magic in this – it is just that confidence helps me stay more relaxed and I fish systematically and with more control. When my confidence is low I cast clumsily with less accuracy and fail to cover the water effectively. Having faith in the fly helps a great deal, it makes fishing more enjoyable as time is spent in keen anticipation. An understanding of how a fly incites a sea trout to rise can take away some of the magic and mystery but it can lead to greater sense of self belief, enjoyment and success. In this section I intend to examine the design and creation of a range of flies I have found to be confidence boosting.

I am in awe of those who can fish a limited range of patterns throughout the season. The professional who taught me to tie flies, confessed to having one customer who fished just one pattern throughout the year for trout, sea trout, salmon and grayling – he just changed sizes. The pattern was the Black Pennel. It is a favourite fly and a pattern that is a safe choice when no other pattern suggests itself but I could not rely upon one fly alone. One of the key aspects of fly-fishing is its versatility and being able to change the cast and adapt to conditions is one of its main strengths. Also I like to experiment and am constantly trying to find the pattern that cannot fail! I tie variations and varieties of all manner of manner of flies but at the end of each season I tidy up my fly boxes and remove those experiments that have failed and these join a growing collection in a bowl on my study windowsill. Gradually I find that I am beginning to reduce my experimentation and am falling back on a small selection of favourites in which I have a high degree of confidence.

Tying my own flies is, for me, an integral part of the fishing. I commend this practice to other fishermen as it adds significantly to the degree of satisfaction to be gained. If new to the craft of fly tying I recommend joining one of the many evening classes devoted to this. They help appreciably with mastery of the basic techniques and provide enjoyable opportunities for exchanging ideas and information.

A number of fishing writers have explored the concept of the 'fly' and put forward the proposition that most of the hooks with fur, feather, tinsel and plastic attached that we now use to catch fish should be termed lures and not flies. The argument follows the thread that the term 'fly' should be restricted to those patterns that attempt to imitate insects that 'fly'. Most of those who support this argument agree that the patterns that represent the water born stages of the fly (nymphs) may also be so termed but all other patterns should be termed

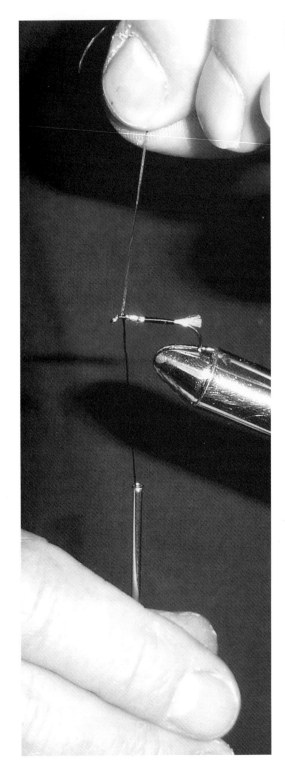

DATE	RIVER	BEAT	CONDITIONS
August 1991	Plym	Shaugh	Falling spate – clearing fast

NOTES

Having caught fish (spinning) that were full of slugs I tried to create an imative pattern based upon a woolly worm. This took nothing when fished upstream but when fished down and across as an attractor it took two schoolies.

FISH CAUGHT	2 sea trout 1lb 1 oz and 10 oz	FLY/LURE	Size 10 Olive Wooly B.

DATE	RIVER	BEAT	CONDITIONS
July 1992	Plym	Shaugh	Falling spate – visibility one metre

NOTES

I caught fish earlier in the week that had taken small olive nymphs and as similar conditions had returned I tried fishing with a small leaded nymph. I managed to hook one fish in the tail of Mac's pool by lifting the rod and inducing a take. The schoolie had an empty stomach

FISH CAUGHT	1 sea trout 1lb 4 oz	FLY/LURE	Size 14 olive nymph

DATE	RIVER	BEAT	CONDITIONS
June 1998	Walkham	Magpie	Falling spate – clearing fast

NOTES

The river seemed full of running peal and when fishing downstream with a short line I was getting follows but no takes on a size 8 Mallard and Silver. I was unable to fish 'fine and far off' because of the cover and in desperation changed to a small Greenwell's spider. Immediately I was catching small browns and took a brace of sea trout over the deeper runs.

FISH CAUGHT	2 sea trout 1lb 10oz and 2lb 2 oz.	FLY/LURE	Size 12 Greenwell's spider.

DATE	RIVER	BEAT	CONDITIONS
June 1997	Walkham	Magpie	Falling spate – clearing fast

NOTES

The river was clearing fast and I caught just a few suicidal browns when fishing down and across. I walked down to the bottom of the beat and worked back up with a Gold Ribbed Hares Ear on a long shank 12 with a lead shot glued on the 'head'. Took a large brown just above the bridge and a fine sea trout in the run below the Outfall Pool.

FISH CAUGHT	Brown trout 1lb 12 oz. Sea trout 2lb 2 oz.	FLY/LURE	Size 12 long shank GRHE leaded.

lures. Lures are patterns that represent no specific flying insect but create the impression of something alive and edible that triggers the fishes feeding instincts and act as 'attractors'. For the sake of simplicity, in this chapter I am going to use the term 'fly' without qualification. I hope those who hold the view that there should be some separation will forgive me.

I introduce this argument not because I am particularly interested in the semantics but before describing the 'flies' I use I want to think once again about why a sea trout rises to a 'fly'. Sea trout as we know, rarely feed once they return to fresh water. A fish that is not feeding is unlikely to respond to imitative patterns and methods and so it could be deduced that fishing for sea trout with these methods is unlikely to reap great rewards. Traditional sea trout patterns are 'attractor' patterns and my fly boxes, are dominated by 'flies' of this type but I also tie and use 'imitative' patterns. I use them because there are times when I find they are better lures than the brighter flies that were designed as such.

I have caught a small number of sea trout with evidence of feeding in their stomachs and I have on occasions, tried patterns that imitate the items eaten, specifically small nymphs, caterpillars and slugs. The patterns have all caught fish but not with any consistency. It may be a coincidence but all the fish that have been caught on these imitative patterns have not eaten anything resembling the item the fly was intended to represent. Most fish had not eaten anything at all. These experiences have persuaded me to treat 'imitative' patterns as 'attractors' and fish them accordingly.

The 'induced take' is a long used and well-established method of taking brown trout. The successful method requires a wet fly or nymph to be cast upstream of a trout and as it is brought back with the current the rod is raised to lift the fly just before it reaches the fish. The trout sees an approaching item appear to come to life and move away - before it can move out of reach the fish pounces. The 'induced take' can also tempt fish whose inclination is not to feed.

In clear water, imitative patterns are more successful than attractors because, I believe, they are less visible and may not seen by the fish until they comes within striking range. The 'induced take' works for sea trout as the fish tends to ignores a small item of riverbed debris trundling with the current until it enters its strike zone when it comes to life and instincts are triggered. If the fish ignores the offering - it is not likely to be worried and you may have the opportunity to try again.

Success with an upstream fly is largely a matter of knowing the water and careful delivery but it also requires the use of a fly that it is not too easily seen. A weighted imitative fly cast upstream and brought back through the pebbles and gullies with occasional lifts will create an effect that can fool a fish or two. This is a challenging method and requires some practice. I recommend it whole-heartedly but do not expect instant results.

Sometimes the fly will be hit as soon as it hits the water. If the fly lands in the fish's window/ strike zone this will sometimes incite it to rise – especially if the fly makes a small 'plop' on hitting the water. In clear water the entry of a weighted fly can frighten fish off but leaded patterns can be an advantage when fishing the quiet runs and eddies during a spate.

Although I enjoy experimenting and trying to take sea trout using innovative methods, I find I employ a traditional down and across wet fly method for much of my sea trout fishing. When there is colour in the river I cast across and downstream and allow my flies to drift around with a varied retrieve. The same method and

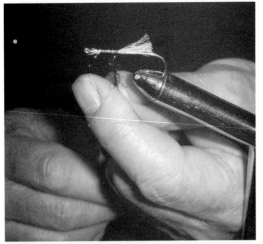

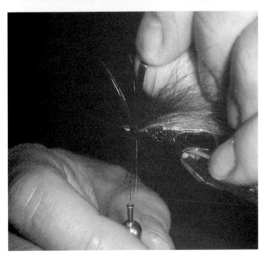

DATE	RIVER	BEAT	CONDITIONS
June 2002	Tavy	Abbey	Falling spate – opaque water

NOTES
Fished up stream with a gold head. Raised three fish in the quiet water against the far bank – all three fish hit the fly immediately after it hit the water – must have been attracted by the splash. Two landed

FISH CAUGHT	2 sea trout 2lb 10oz and 1lb 2 oz.	FLY/LURE	Size 10 Gold Head GRHE

DATE	RIVER	BEAT	CONDITIONS
June 2005	Tavy	Middle	Low clear 15 C

NOTES
Low water, clear sky. Fished consistently with a large black and silver fly which had provided sport the previous week. Fish were showing and crashing around the pool but I could not get any interest Tried changing lines to no effect. Exchanged notes with the other rod as I was leaving and found that he had a taken a brace on a size 10 fly. I should have read the signs and changed down to a smaller fly.

FISH CAUGHT	0	FLY/LURE	Size 6 Silver Special

DATE	RIVER	BEAT	CONDITIONS
July 2005	Tavy	Middle	Low clear 13C

NOTES
Low water, full moon and broken sky. Temperatures falling to 13 degrees. Fished hard and persistently with all manner of flies on a floating line until 1.00am with just two pulls. Tried a popper before I left the pool. Four savage takes in three casts but each fish was lost after thrashing briefly on the surface.

FISH CAUGHT	0	FLY/LURE	Size 4 Popper

DATE	RIVER	BEAT	CONDITIONS
July 2004	Tavy	Middle	Low clear 13C

NOTES
Low water and overcast sky. It grew dark quite early. Fished the Run with no success just after dark and arrived at the pool to find the other rod had taken a 2lb fish on a fly with chemical 'lite' attached. I followed him through and took 2 schoolies. Returning to the run I had a third my companion persevering with the high tech fly had no further luck. I left him to it and I gather he continued until very late with no more takes.

FISH CAUGHT	2 sea trout 1lb 2 oz and 1 of 12 oz	FLY/LURE	Size 10 Half Silver

variations of it I employ at night and when I am operating under the cover of darkness.

When the water is carrying some colour I will fish downstream with a range of patterns depending upon the speed, depth and colour of the water. I almost always fish a single fly in the day and try to work it with precision. It is easier to control a lone fly while drifting it around the ledges and snags. I try to select a fly that will not be seen by the fish before it enters its strike zone. I cast beyond where I expect the fish to lie let it drift with the current for 50 centimetres or so and then lift it, drift and lift. The clearer the water the smaller and duller my selection.

When darkness falls I usually employ similar flies to those I use on a clearing river in the daytime but a size or two larger. I fish 'attractor' patterns for most of the season and invariably employ a dropper. These are tied on single hooks. I add the second fly partly to bring a slightly different pattern into play but also because I am not able to fish with the same degree of precision at night. The two flies enable me to cover a larger area with each cast and it increases my chances of placing a fly in a fish's strike zone. In the dark I am less worried that a fish will see both flies and be put off. About 25 % of my fish come to the dropper.

During the darker nights and especially during the early season I am using attractor patterns that are fairly large in size (6s). As the season progresses I reduce the size of the fly (10s) and may use tiny imitative patterns (12/14s) on moonlit nights. The reason for this is that on the bright nights the fish's visual range extends while its strike range remains constant. A failure to connect on light nights is because the fish sees the fly when it is too far away for a 'snatch and grab'. On these nights smaller traditional wet flies of a duller design will produce results - 'Invicta', March Brown, or Black and Peacock Spider.

Occasionally if the standard approach has drawn a blank I will use wake flies – 'muddlers' or 'poppers'. These often have a remarkable effect and will be hit by small brown trout two, three or more times as the cast sweeps across the current. Larger sea trout will break the surface and swirl at the wake fly more times than they will take it. I think sea trout respond to the surface lure at night as they would to a large spinner in the day.

I am often reluctant to use a surface-lure as I think it may disturb the pool and affect the rest of the night's fishing and so it tends to be used as a last resort. But it adds another weapon to the armoury. On nights when I am especially indecisive I will take three different fly boxes to the river, and usually have a film canister with a few poppers in my pocket.

All my flies began as traditional or established patterns but have been adapted and developed to the extent that the origins may unidentifiable. Although I am ever experimenting and devising new patterns I aim to create a small range in different sizes that will meet most conditions. I cannot resist tying variations but when I look at my creations there are many common factors. The fly is only going to be seen for a 'split second' before it is attacked or rejected. It must have a profile that instantly looks like something living. The material used to construct the fly must have some translucency and some movement to enhance this illusion. Finally 'attractor' patterns need some 'glitter'.

All my patterns have a 'hackle' behind the head of the fly. Usually a black cock hackle is used and a feather is selected that when wound around the hook the tips almost touch the point of the hook. Behind the hackle I often create a 'shoulder' very much like the 'thorax' of a nymph. This is constructed with dubbed fur and I find I am increasingly using artificial materials with some 'sparkle'. This short shoulder helps create a lifelike profile and when

DATE	RIVER	BEAT	CONDITIONS
August 2005	Tavy	Lower	Low clear- cold 10 C

NOTES

Low water and clear sky. Northerly component to the wind and not feeling overconfident. Found another rod on the river tackled up with a micro 'lite' fly. This glowed in the dark which he claimed could not fail. Despite this he chose to fish the most favoured stand on the main pool - so I fished the run. Subsequently I had three takes and landed two fish despite marginal conditions. The other rod was fishless. Temperatures were continuing to drop and so I left early with my brace.

FISH CAUGHT	1lb 4 oz and 14 oz	FLY/LURE	Size 10 Special

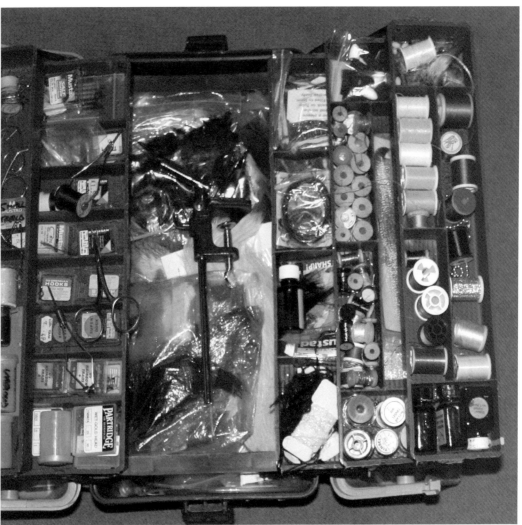

teased out helps add movement. I am not sure how much sea trout 'hear' flies moving through the water and to what degree the turbulence created by the fly generates sound or vibration. A fly with a hackle and a rough body may well create more 'noise' than a slim fly and I incorporate the dubbing shoulder partly with this in mind. Behind the shoulder, the main body is often created with a shiny material. I used to use flat tinsel but now use one of the artificial wing materials that I varnish over rather than rib with fine wire.

I often dispense with a wing on smaller flies but the larger lures generally incorporate a wing of black or blue hair. The wing helps create a sense of movement and imparts life to the fly but it is difficult to effect this with wings of less than a centimetre and if the wing extends beyond the bend of the hook it can loop under the bend when casting and destroy the desired effect.

It is now possible to tie into the dressing material that does 'glow in the dark' and even small chemical lights. I have experimented with luminous material both by day and night with little success. Although I incorporate a small tag or tail of 'day glow' floss into some of my night fishing patterns I have abandoned the luminous material. I think it causes the fish to see the fly before it reaches its attack zone and it is subsequently rejected.

For similar reasons I have not bothered with the chemical lights. Although I have seen fellow fishermen take fish on them, on the same nights I have out fished them with more traditional patterns.

I know fishermen who cut the tails off 'shop bought' patterns before using them for sea trout. It is a common belief that sea trout nibble at the tails of flies and do not take them cleanly. Without this extension to the dressing they are more likely to grab the whole. I am unconvinced by this and while I have seen sea trout follow

flies while daytime fishing they do not nip at the tails. Many predators attack bait fish by swimming hard into them and then returning to pick off the injured. Sea trout can be seen doing this when fishing a large spinner or fly in the daytime. Sometimes the surface is broken and the rise of the fish is seen but there is no solid take just a small tap on the line. Sea trout will often 'hit' big flies without opening their mouths and when this happens small 'taps' on the line are often felt. I have seen this happen in the daytime. Most of the taps will come from undersize fish. Small par and trout that are often too small to get the fly in their mouths will attack a sea trout fly in the dark. They can create the impression that a larger fish is nibbling and I am sure that 99% of the 'short takes' reported by sea trout anglers are in fact fish too small to engulf the hook.

Sea trout that have been induced to rise to a fly will hit it with a closed mouth or grab it firmly. A tail on the fly makes no difference. If the fish are 'coming short' and hitting the fly with their noses it is always a case of using too large a fly. It is difficult to determine if this is what is being felt when there are small knocks on the line a small fly (10 or less) cannot be 'torpedoed' that easily and is usually engulfed or ignored. Changing down a couple of sizes will catch fish when this is happening it may be the intended sea trout, but it may also be small 'nuisance' fish. Sea trout fishermen on the Tamar tend to change up a size when being plagued by par to reduce the chances of hooking them. On the often clearer Tavy I have not found this to be a helpful tactic.

A 'tail' on a sea trout fly creates some resistance, and therefore some lift at the end of the dressing. It helps the fly remain on an even keel and resists the tendency to hang vertically in the water - the heavier bend of the hook can cause the tail to drop when the retrieve is very slow. The tail also adds to the lifelike effect of the fly.

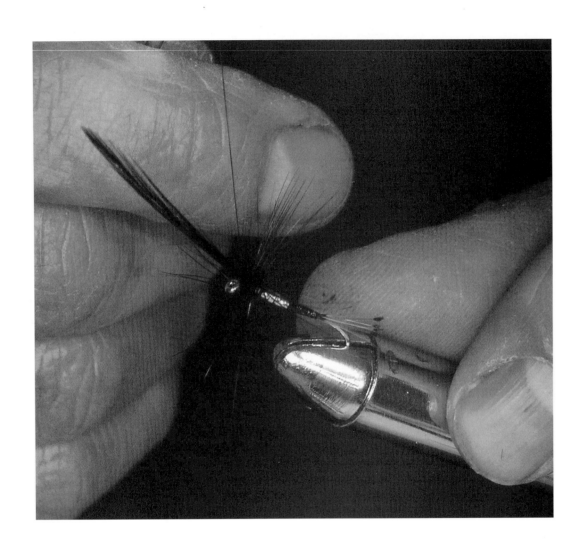

I include tails on all of my sea trout flies. Smaller patterns tied on standard wet fly hooks of size 10 or smaller may have a traditional tippet of golden pheasant and this will extend beyond the bend. Flies tied on long shank 10s or larger will have a tail created from floss that is no longer than the radius of the bend of the hook and does not extend beyond it. Flies for use at night may have 'tags' of daylight fluorescent floss.

The hook that is employed is an important factor. While most hooks manufactured for fly tying do the job they are intended for very well in that they hook and hold fish, the variations available do effect presentation and this is important. Standard wet fly hooks are very good for day time flies but I am not sure that the down-turned eye has any real benefit and I would prefer straight eyed hooks if they were readily available in the gauge and sizes I prefer.

At night I am unable to be certain of the exact location of my flies as they are swept with the current and as I am always fishing around ledges, shoals, rocks and other underwater obstructions I find a heavy, wide gape hook frequently becomes caught on the bottom. A long shank allows me to use a fly of the same proportions but with the narrower gape. When this is partly masked by a hackle it gets snagged less often.

My weighted flies are now tied onto the 'gold head' hooks that have been designed to facilitate the threading of a small bead onto the hook. These have a small barb but a wide gape and have proved excellent hookers. As the weight makes them fish 'upside down' the wide gape does not cause them to catch on the bottom any more than other hooks. In fact as the weight causes the fly to invert I find I have fewer problems with getting caught up and can fish the flies very slowly when I need to.

I have experimented with 'silver' plated hooks produced for sea anglers as these enable me to dispense with a tinsel body. These are very good fish holders and enable me to tie effective flies but the hooks are not available in sizes smaller than 4. I find I can get away with a shorter dressing and still create an attractive fly but it is difficult to fish it as slowly as I would like around the shallow tails and ledges. Stainless steel hooks designed for saltwater fly fisherman are usually too heavy a gauge and have points that blunt easily. I am worried about leaving a non-rusting hook in a fish but If there were some size 8, 10 and 12 versions of the 'silver' plated 'Viking' patterns available I would be tempted to try them.

The following patterns have become favourites and dominate my fly boxes. They are mostly hybrids and I encourage those who experiment with them to continue their development and evolution. There is nothing sacred in the patterns and I claim no copyright on the designs. Anyone is free to try them and produce their own versions for personal use. Each has been developed from an existing pattern or patterns and where I can credit the origins of the fly I began with I have endeavoured to do so.

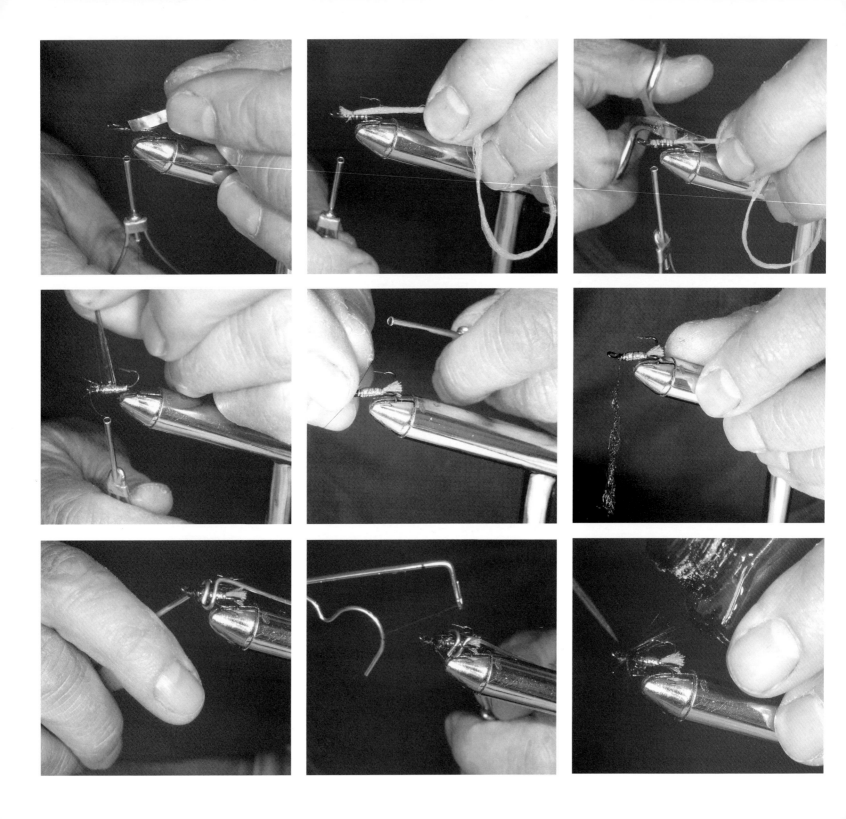

Some favourite patterns

1. Bob's Special

The 'Special' is a derivative of Moc Morgan's 'Moc's Cert and the body has been influenced by Dave Tait's reservoir flies. The Special has been created in blue, green and orange versions. It is the fly I use most frequently at night – usually it is as a dropper. I have often given some to other anglers who have been using other patterns with limited success and they have named this fly.

HOOK:	Size 12 – 8 (mainly 10) standard or long shank
THREAD:	Black
TAIL:	Fluorescent floss (short) - usually orange but sometimes red or green
BODY:	'Flashabou' varnished over – mainly blue but sometimes orange or green
THORAX:	Black dubbing
WING:	None
HACKLE:	Black cock

Instructions
   a) Tie in a length of fluorescent floss and trim to line up with the end of the hook.
   b) Tie in 4 strands of Flashabou tinsel and wind around the shank towards the head stopping 5 mm from the head.
   c) Tie off and trim Flashabou, cover with 1 or 2 coats of varnish and leave to dry
   d) When dry – dub a short (2 turns) thorax/shoulder with black dubbing.
   e) Select a black hackle that when wound comes close to the point of the hook. 'Henny' hackles from the side of a cape are good. Tie in and wind 4 times around the hook.
   Whip finish and varnish the head.

2. The Bluebottle

The fly is a 'Special' tied on a small salmon treble or double hook. A leaded under-body gives it a fatter profile and helps it 'plop' when it hits the water. The blue or green versions look a little like bluebottle flies - hence the title. It is a daytime fly and is fished down and across in coloured water if the flow does not demand a heavy tube fly. It will often take salmon. Sea trout often respond as it enters the water and may hit it before the line is taut so it is important to be ready for this.

3. The (Winged) Special

The silver special was developed to include a hair wing and to utilise the silver shank of a plated hook thus avoiding the tedious varnishing of the body. I have since become worried about using non rusting hooks and have changed to hooks with a bright anodised coating. It has become a night-time favourite especially in the first half of the season and on the darkest nights of early summer. The saltwater hooks have an extremely good hold and have led to less fish lost but the larger gape means they catch on the ledges and cannot always be fished as slowly as I would like. I use it over deeper water when the river is running clear but above summer levels. I start the season with this fly but perhaps fish it for too long and should change down to a smaller pattern by June. In the sea it has proved a good bass fly!

HOOK:	Viking size 6
THREAD:	Black
TAIL:	Fluorescent floss (short) - pink, orange or green
BODY:	Front third – sparkle dubbing – black/peacock
WING:	Black (over blue or orange) squirrel or fox. Under wing is barred with a felt tip pen.
HACKLE:	Black cock (Red natural cock with orange body)

Instructions
   a) Tie in a length of pink fluorescent floss for the tail. The tail begins half way down the shank and ends before the start of the bend. It is really a short secondary wing.
   b) Dub a short body/thorax of black sparkle dubbing or similar.
   c) Tie in a wing of black over blue or orange hair. The wing extends to the end of the hook but not beyond.
   d) Select a black hackle that when wound comes close to the point of the hook. Tie in and wind 4 times around the hook.
   e) Whip finish and varnish head.
   f) Put 'bar' markings on the under wing using a permanent black felt tip pen. This will wash out after prolonged use but the marking can be repeated if necessary.

4. The Half Silver

This is now my favourite point fly and has become very successful. It was inspired by a still water pattern called the Sinfoil Fry. At one time I used the 'Sinfoil' regularly for fishing around shallow ledges and snags where a long shank 12 was less likely than a standard 8 to get caught up. I have since adapted the pattern, giving it a full hackle and a tail. I substitute mylar tubing for the flat silver and varnish over the body rather than covering it with the polythene of the original pattern.

HOOK:	8 – 12 (long shank – straight eye)
THREAD:	Black
TAIL:	GP Tippett
BODY:	Front half silver mylar tubing - back half black silk. Varnished over
RIB:	None
WING:	None – on larger sizes a slim black hair wing can be added
HACKLE:	Black cock

Instructions

a)   Catch the silk and tie in 4 or so GP tippet fibres for the tail
b)   Cut a section of mylar tubing a little short of the length of the body and tease out the string filling.
c)   Carefully slide the tube over the eye and position on the shank.
d)   Tie in the tail end of the tube and tie in the tail of tippets.
e)   Finish the rear half of the body with overlapping turns of silk to cover half the mylar.
f)   Whip or use half hitches to tie off the silk half way down the body.
g)   Catch in the silk at the head and fasten the tube at the head with minimum turns. Trim off the excess mylar.
h)   Varnish the body, avoiding the tail tippets and put aside to dry.
i)   Select a black hackle with fibres a little on the short side. 'Henny' hackles from the side of a cape are good. Tie in and wind 4 times around the hook.
j)   Clip off the end of the hackle, whip finish and varnish.

5. Midnight popper

This is a wake fly that will cause an otherwise dead pool to come to life. It will provoke many more hits than takes but is useful to try before heading for home on an otherwise blank night. It can be fished down and across or cast upstream and brought back just a little faster than the current. A good fly to cast upstream into the eddies behind the necks of pools. It must be kept moving as fish will lose interest as soon as it falls still. Warning: this fly does cause considerable disturbance and is not a fly to use if you or others intend to continue fishing the pool with more subtle methods for the rest of the night.

HOOK:	Viking Saltwater size 4
THREAD:	Black
TAIL:	None
BODY:	None
WING:	Black squirrel or fox
HACKLE:	Black cock
HEAD:	Estafoam cylinder (booby eye material)

Instructions

a)   Take a 10 mm diameter bar of 'estafoam', the type sold for 'Booby Eyes' and cut a section about 15mm. Pierce this with a heavy needle from the circular end.
b)   Place the hook in the vice and catch in the silk winding it down 15mm from the eye and make a half hitch.
c)   Cover the silk with adhesive (superglue) and slide the foam cylinder over the eye and down to cover the silk>
d)   Tie down the (bend) end of the foam - pulling it down to create a bell shaped head to the fly.
e)   Tie in the wing immediately behind the foam head>
f)   Tie in the hackle and give it at least 4 turns.
g)   Tie off with half hitches or whip finish behind the head.
h)   Varnish over the thread behind the head (note some varnishes may affect the foam – try first)>

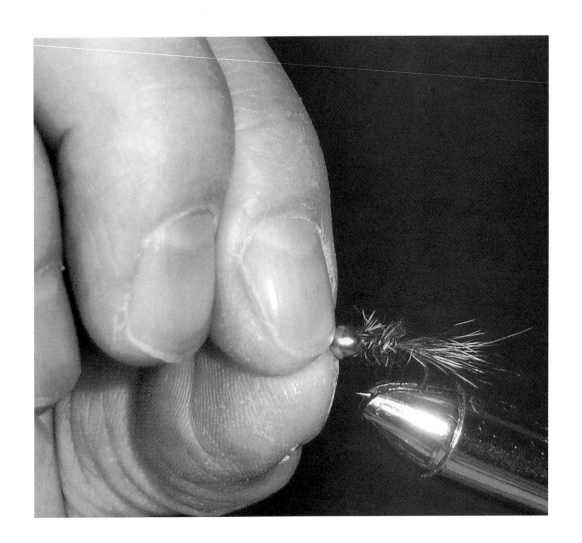

6. The 'Gold Shoulder'

This fly is a derivative of the 'Gold Head' and was devised as an alternative to a leaded nymph for upstream fishing in daytime conditions. The brass bead is placed behind the hackle instead of at the head as in the original. I use two versions – a Gold Ribbed Hare's Ear for clear water and a Black Pennel-influenced version with a silver bead, for coloured water. The black version has taken summer salmon as well as the sea trout for which it was intended and is sometimes used at night when the water is clearing but remains high.

HOOK:	Gold Head Hook 8 – 12
THORAX:	Gold (brass) bead - (Black verion - silver bead)
THREAD:	Black
TAIL:	Hare fibres - (Black version - GP Tippett)
BODY:	Hare's Ear - (Black version - fine black dubbing)
RIB:	Fine Gold
WING:	None
HACKLE:	Dark hen - (Black version - black hen)

Instructions: As I have experienced difficulty with the brass bead moving down the body when casting the traditional 'Goldhead' the tying of this fly is a little special.

a) Thread a brass bead onto the hook.
b) Catch and wind black thread in spaced turns down and back up the shank.
c) Tie in and wind four times a hen hackle.
d) Whip finish the head of the fly.
e) Apply adhesive (super glue) thinly to shank and move bead up to behind the hackle.
f) Catch the thread behind the bead and tie in the tail.
g) Tie in the rib.
h) Dub as slim as possible body behind the bead - a slightly tapered body with black dubbing.
i) Scrub body with Velcro or tease out dubbing with a needle.
j) Tighten rib if necessary and tie off behind the bead.
k) Varnish the head and the tying off behind the bead.

Chapter 8

The Grilse

The rivers of West Devon hold brown trout, sea trout and salmon. Brown trout and sea trout are technically the same species but the salmon, although closely related, is in many ways a very different creature. I include a section on salmon in this collection of notes as my sea trout fishing does overlap with some salmon fishing and I want to stress the differences between the species.

There is a idea that the salmon is the 'King' of fish and superior to the sea trout. Whilst I would not hold that the salmon is an inferior fish I am not convinced that it is in any way better than the sea trout. The only advantage a salmon has over the sea trout is that it is usually bigger. In all other respects it does not seem to surpass the sea trout. Out of preference I focus on sea trout throughout the summer months. On my rivers they are more plentiful, more challenging, and early season sea trout make much better eating. I am also conscious that the salmon is practically an endangered species and we should be accord them some special consideration.

Once September has arrived, the leaves on the oaks harden and rustle noticeably in the wind. This seems to signal that for this season, sea trout fishing has passed its best. From this point until the end of the season I target salmon. Officially I could continue to cast for sea trout until the end of the month but I do not want to harass and risk injury to fish that are soon to spawn. Some clubs forbid the killing of sea trout in September but I have the choice. Late sea trout do not make good eating, mature fish will be bland and tasteless and all those caught at this time are returned. But when the summer sport comes to an end, I am always reluctant

to hang up my rods for the winter and so some afternoons teasing autumn run salmon provide an enjoyable way to finish the season.

Each summer I hook a salmon while fishing for sea trout and later in the season, I may hook a sea trout while fishing for salmon. All takes are welcome, they confirm the health of the water and can liven up the day. But I am often disappointed to hook a salmon when I am targeting sea trout - it seems a matter of lucky rather than skilful fishing.

Sea trout will rise to a lure presented for salmon and vice versa. It is possible to use identical methods and lures to take both species (on the same day) but pursuing both simultaneously presents some difficulties. A greater degree of success will be found by targeting one species or the other and adapting tactics accordingly. The difference in tactics is very subtle but very significant and on rivers where every fish, sea trout or salmon is hard won, trying to 'hedge your bets' by using hybrid methods can lead to an enjoyable day but an empty bag. Before taking a cast I recommend a decision be taken on whether to fish for salmon or whether to target sea trout. I hope that this chapter may help others consider this and subsequently enjoy their fishing all the more.

The decision can be made pool-by-pool, or even cast-by-cast but as I have indicated - I tend to split the fishing season into two. The rivers I fish do not produce many spring salmon, but there are a few summer grilse. Autumn runs of salmon can be generous and so I devote the summer months to the quest for sea trout, my preferred species and from the end of August to the end of the season I fish for salmon.

DATE	RIVER	BEAT	CONDITIONS
August 2002	River Tavy	Middle	Low clear 16C

NOTES

Began fishing in the 'dimpsey' but it was too early and in my impatience I had probably put down the fish in the pool. I thought I should rest it for a while and so walked up to have a few casts in the run into the pool. It was now completely dark and was soon rewarded by a tentative 'pluck' in the eddies at the end of the rush down to the pool. I lifted the rod and saw the surface break in what light there was and I found I had a fish on.

The fish was a good one and fought doggedly. It broke the surface with some violent thrashes but no leaps and no wild runs. It didn't seem like a sea trout somehow. Eventually it was netted and as I reached down into the net to grasp the fish I felt scales – not the smooth skin of a sea trout. I put a torch on the fish and confirmed I had caught a salmon.

The fish was bagged and I continued down to The Run taking two peal before I reached the main pool. I carried on fishing the pool for another hour without a touch. Fish were showing and they had been taking in The Run - I must have disturbed them by my early start but I was satisfied with my catch.

FISH CAUGHT	1 Salmon 6lb 2 Sea Trout 14oz	FLY/LURE	Size 10 Special.

DATE	RIVER	BEAT	CONDITIONS
August 2000	River Tavy	Middle	Falling spate 15C

NOTES

Fishing downstream after a spate I was hoping for a fresh-run peal. The 'hot spots' on the beat failed to provide a take and before going home I thought I would have a cast or two for a summer salmon and so I changed flies and set out to tackle a couple of the pools and runs once again.

In these conditions I have found salmon in the necks of pools and so concentrated my efforts here. I approached the first run into a pool and began to cast. A cast or two and I would have moved on had I been expecting sea trout but a salmon was the goal and so I gave it a good five minutes. I cast, allowed the fly to hang in the current and cast again but this time I gave line allowed the fly to drift and then held back. The next time I reached out with the rod so that once the fly had swept across to the limit of its travel and was on the dangle it turned back and moved away.

I entertained myself by trying variations of working the fly as it swept the lie and eventually a fish rose and took the fly. I cannot remember what trick was being employed at the time but a 5lb grilse came to the net before too long.

FISH CAUGHT	1 Salmon 5 lb	FLY/LURE	Bluebottle 14 treble

There are exceptions and during summer spates I may change tactics to explore some specific lies in the hope of finding a taking grilse. This does not happen often but having fished through a pool for sea trout with no success and if no one else is fishing down behind me I may change approach and try again but with salmon in mind.

If fishing a pool twice in succession, as described above, it is imperative to fish for the sea trout first. A salmon will often ignore the first fly it sees and subsequently hit the next lure it is offered but a sea trout having seen and refused any lure in daylight will not respond to any subsequent flies, spinners or plugs. It needs a significant rest period before it can be induced to rise again. I sometimes return to places where I have raised sea trout before leaving the river and give it an optimistic cast or two. I very rarely take fish on these occasions but cannot always resist giving it a try. On a couple of occasions I have returned to a spot where I have risen a sea trout to find a salmon was sharing the lie and it was this fish that rose and took the lure. The sea trout is 'twice shy'.

Sea trout look so much like salmon that they are often confused and mistaken for each other. In addition to the visual similarities, their paths cross in Devon rivers during the fishing seasons. Several times I have encountered fishermen carrying large stale sea trout, fish of 6 – 8lb, along the banks of the Plym happy in the belief that they have caught a winter salmon. This frequently happens and a local chap, who perhaps should have known better, was prosecuted for taking sea trout out of season despite claiming he 'thought it was a salmon'. One August night I caught a very small grilse of 4 lb that caused some debate amongst fellow fisherman. Many argued that it was a sea trout but subsequently scale readings proved it was a salmon.

There are many ways of telling the difference and this is much better described in other publications but I can usually tell as soon as it is hooked. A glance at the scales of the fish confirms its identity once on the bank. Salmon scales are distinctly larger than those of a similar sized sea trout and the difference can be felt. Even in the dark the feel of a salmon is distinct from that of a sea trout – you can feel the individual scales on the former.

Apart from the similarities and differences in the look of the fish salmon and sea trout behave in different ways - they often demonstrate a preference for different parts of the stream, they certainly take a lure differently and fight with their own style but they differ mostly in what may be called temperament. It is an understanding of the fish's 'temperament' that allows the angler to trigger its predatory instincts. Time can otherwise be 'wasted' pursuing sea trout with salmon tactics and vice versa. Greater success is more likely to fall to those who recognise the differences and respond accordingly.

In Chapter 3 I describe the lies where sea trout may be found and salmon are like sea trout in that they need well-oxygenated flows, security and to conserve energy. Salmon and sea trout may be found lying side by side but if you are given opportunity to observe both species populating a pool you will see that the salmon will take up different positions to the majority of sea trout. Not surprisingly for what is often a much bigger fish it will favour deeper water.

When it is relaxed and feeling safe a salmon will drift back to the tails and the margins of the pool, very much like a sea trout. If there is some cover from an overhanging bank or vegetation so much the better. Here in the shallows the salmon is able to 'take it easy' – it does not need to fight the flow. In the margins of smaller streams a salmon will sometimes be found with its head tucked under a rock or root and its tail stuck out for all to see!

DATE	RIVER	BEAT	CONDITIONS
August 1991	River Walkham	Magpie	Low water slight stain.

NOTES

Fishing upstream with a weighted nymph I had taken and released several browns but was hoping to entice a sea trout. I cast my fly up into the head and as it drifted back to where I thought there might be a fish I raised the rod and tried to induce a take.

In the Chip Shop I made a poor cast and the nymph was trundling back through the deep slate groove rather than the pebbly shoulder of the pool. I raised the rod anyway and was surprised to feel a heavy fish responding. For a moment I thought it was a good sea trout but it showed itself to be a fresh grilse. It was a lively one and took some handling on the trout rod and at one stage got behind me and down stream into the run. I had to follow and eventually it tired and I was able to hand tail it adjacent to the old mine shaft.

FISH CAUGHT	1 salmon 5lb	FLY/LURE	Size 12 leaded GRHE Nymph.

DATE	RIVER	BEAT	CONDITIONS
September 2001	Tavy	Middle	Overnight rain – river falling some colour. 17C

NOTES

I began fishing at the top of the run with a small copper tube with a pearl and blue dressing. This was fished across the fast water at the very top of the run as I have had fish take almost at my ankles here. Alas it was not the case today and I continued down casting to drop into the gully alongside a protruding rock.

On the second cast I had a take and still in sea trout form I struck and the fly came back to me. A salmon? If so I had not allowed it to properly take the fly. I adjusted my stand and began to cast again and again working down to where the take had come. As I hit the spot the fish came again. I dropped the rod waited briefly and then felt for the fish. It was still there I tightened and was into a lively salmon. This headed for the rapids upstream but then turned and ran downstream. This seemed to take all of its energy and I was able to lead it to a place where I could grasp it by the tail and lift it out of the water. The treble was well driven into the scissors and required pliers to remove it.

FISH CAUGHT	1 Salmon 7lb	FLY/LURE	1" Blue and Pearl Tube

Shallow water lies of a foot or so (30cm) where the flow is gentle can make suitable resting places but are not good salmon taking places - it may be that salmon require a little more pace in the flow or space to attack a lure. It may be that when resting the predatory instincts are completely turned off.

In spates, fish seek out the shelter of the margins but may enthusiastically attack a lure despite the lack of depth. May be the increased speed of water makes the fish more alert and ready to attack. The faster flow of the river in spate will enable it to power forward with greater ease but having been pushed out of a comfortable lie by the fresh current it may be in a heightened state of consciousness.

In low and clear water I find salmon can be sometimes 'woken up' and tempted out of a shallow, resting lie to follow a lure. If then it adopts a mid stream position it may well rise and take the lure on the next cast. But in all conditions a salmon lying in or near the main flow through a pool it is more likely to rise to a lure. In September when I am trying to avoid hooking stale sea trout I fish the streamy water over clean slate bottoms as at this time the sea trout will be populating the pebbly gravel runs.

The very sill or tail of a deep pool is a good place to find both salmon and sea trout in high water. On these occasions the increased and turbulent flow across through shallow water lies make them good taking places for both species. Some colour in the water also makes the fisherman less visible to the fish. These are good places for summer grilse when the river is in spate and sea trout also like these places. The sea trout will hang back further than the salmon and will often lie just beyond the tail in the broken water just downstream. Sometimes when the river is 'up' I will fish a pool with a fast moving lure for sea trout and if the fancy takes me change flies and fish it once again and more slowly, for salmon.

Salmon have a preference for a clean rock bottom and throughout the Tavy and its tributaries the deep gullies of slate washed clean by the healthy flows are places to find taking salmon. This, I learnt from Jeffrey Bluett who in his excellent book Sea Trout and Occasional Salmon, notes this characteristic.

There may be many reasons why salmon favour a rock bottom. Perhaps the colour of the West Country slate closely matches the blue/green/grey back of a fresh fish and it feels better camouflaged. Perhaps it is the presence of an even flow of water over the smooth clean rock enables it to hold its station with less effort. Sea trout like gravel and prefer pebbly and broken ground where they can effortlessly hold station in the turbulence around individual stones. Their spotted backs make them more suitable to this background or and their smaller size enables them to take advantage of the micro conditions between the pebbles. The reasons for the different inclinations may be subject to conjecture but the facts are worth noting. It is possible to target either species by selecting where through a pool you choose to fish.

Salmon also differ from sea trout in the way they take a lure. Once in a while I raise a salmon in a place where I anticipate a sea trout to be lying. Too frequently I tighten in a spontaneous reaction and pull the hook from the fish's mouth. This may well happen much more than I realise as only occasionally do I get sufficient a view of the fish to identify it positively.

Although almost every fish is different, when a sea trout takes a lure it generally snatches at the 'bait' and turns away with a swipe of its head. Being smaller it need less room to turn and does so almost immediately. A sudden jerk (or two) is felt and if it is met with like pressure the fish will be well hooked. Any delay in reacting or slack in the line results in the fish spitting out the hard object. A salmon's take is

DATE	RIVER	BEAT	CONDITIONS
August 2002	Tavy	Middle	Low, clear 17C

NOTES

Waiting for it to get dark enough to fish the pool for sea trout lazily wet my flies in the fast water and the top of the pool. I was practising casting and trying to put the waiting time to use. I gradually lengthened my cast until my flies were hanging in the current just where the broken water ends and the flow becomes smooth. Moving the rod tip enabled me to keep the flies hovering and fluttering in the stream. The surface erupted and a large fish took the fly and headed downstream. I followed and later landed a 6lb salmon that had taken the point fly.
I continued down The Run with no further sport but took two good sized peal in the very tail of Big Pool on the same fly. The largest sea trout took almost as long to land as the much bigger salmon.

FISH CAUGHT	1 Salmon 6lb 2 Sea trout 1lb 4oz and 1lb 6 oz	FLY/LURE	Size 10 Black Special

DATE	RIVER	BEAT	CONDITIONS
September 1988	Walkham	Magpie	Falling and clearing after overnight rain

NOTES

Having fished through the pool carefully, my plug was followed by a large fish that did not take. I was not sure if it was a salmon or a large stale sea trout. The fish returned to a lie in the channel against the far bank When it followed my lure across the gravel bank it was possibly too shallow for it to grab the bottom hugging lure. I fished through the pool and then returned to top to fish down again. I let the plug flutter across the deep gullies as long as I could and once more the fish came out and followed it. The next cast I waded out as far as my wellies would allow and cast to my bank allowing the plug to drift out and into the deep channel. This time it took the lure positively and a clean Autumn cock fish was landed in the tail.

FISH CAUGHT	1 Salmon 7 ¾ lb	FLY/LURE	Rapala CD7

sometimes a much gentler affair. It rises to the lure takes it in its mouth and if it has the space, flows casually back to its lie. As it turns the full weight of the fish is felt and this is the time to set the hook. But if the fish has taken the lure in a small pool, between rocks or in one of the narrow gullies favoured by salmon on West Country streams it may continue swimming forward, glide gently downward or just hold station in the stream. The line can go slack or just a slight tap is felt and striking at this stage will result at best in a lightly hooked fish.

When a fish takes a lure the experienced angler will be aware that something is happening to the end of the line. The instinctive strike of a twitchy highly-strung trout fisherman (a group to which I claim membership) is unlikely to hook the fish. Tightening too soon pulls the lure from the salmon's mouth but the salmon is a forgiving creature (unlike the sea trout) and will often give you a second chance. Sea trout fishing must be controlled but it is exciting, fast, instant reaction, one chance stuff while salmon fishing has to be a much more relaxed affair. As I get older it is growing in attraction but forsaking the sea trout for salmon fishing would be like selling the sports car for a stately saloon. I'm not quite ready yet.

At times a deep lying salmon will rise up from the guts on the Tavy and take a subsurface lure like a brown trout. While waiting for dark and the sea trout fishing to begin I will while away a half hour or so playing a fly across the streamy water at the head of a pool. A lie that holds salmon but one that I am unlikely to want to fish after dark. Starting here while it is not quite dark I am unlikely to disturb the fish I aim to catch but as the light fades there is a chance I may raise a salmon.

I discovered this one night when I started sea trout fishing far too early. It was a bright mid summer night and although 'last orders' had long been called it was still light enough to see

across the river and down to the next pool. Patience was wearing thin and I started to fish the flow into the neck of the pool. Standing well back and half-heartedly letting the fly swing across while the daylight faded, the lure was taken by large fish. It immediately turned and headed for the sea eventually breaking me in the next pool down. In the half-light it rolled several times on the surface and was clearly a salmon.

I now frequently fish the neck of the pool in the half-light. Not always has it resulted in a fish on the bank but it has given me some exercise while waiting for the real action after dark. Sea trout and salmon relish the fast water at the head of the pool and will leap and show as dusk arrives. Sea trout seem to dash up to the fast broken water 'for some air', leap and circle back to lie in the slower water but I rarely hook a peal in the fast water after dark. Salmon however will move up to the neck when dusk arrives and stay until daylight. They are often in the mood to rise and a fly drifted slowly across the stream and allowed to hover and flutter over the gullies can induce a take.

Salmon often take a fly 'on the dangle' but it is rare for this to happen with a sea trout. As I have explained in Chapter 3 I believe a sea trout will only be provoked to attack a lure if taken by surprise. Salmon will react likewise but often require a little more time and sometimes like to see the lure several times. They are particularly prone to snapping with frustration at a lure that is being dangled in front of their noses. A sea trout will become irritated by such tactics and will quickly move off or bolt for a secure hiding place.

Occasionally a sea trout will rise and follow a lure that is sweeping across a pool, until it comes to a stop below the angler. If the lure changes direction and continues to move forward sometimes the fish will take but if it stops the sea trout leave the lure and return to

DATE	RIVER	BEAT	CONDITIONS
October 1988	River Walkham	Magpie	River up but falling - peat stained

NOTES

Spinning on a falling river a salmon leapt under my rod from the Chip Shop Pool. I finished fishing through the pool and went back to the top and fished it again and then once more. I continued downstream and met two other fishermen fishing up stream. I did not mention the fish in the 'Chip Shop' but each was a good fisherman and knew it might hold fish in these conditions.

After fishing the lower pools on the beat I returned to the Chip Shop and fished it again three times to no avail. I continued up stream and met the other two who had also fished this tiny pool several times with no luck. They were now leaving and before I did I decided to try the pool again. The river was dropping and it is unlikely that the salmon had run up or down and would try to wait until the next spate under the gouged out bank.

I dropped down a size in plug and fished it again three times. The third time and what may have well been the last cast it took.

The fish made no dramatic runs or leaps but just doggedly bore to the bottom and shook its head but eventually it was pumped to the surface and a bright 7lb salmon was landed.

FISH CAUGHT	1 Salmon 7 ½ lb	FLY/LURE	Rapala CD 7

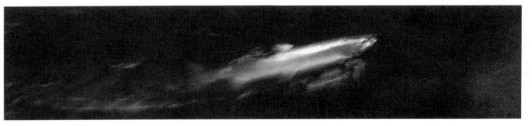

DATE	RIVER	BEAT	CONDITIONS
September 2001	Tavy	Middle	Falling and clearing after overnight rain

NOTES

Took the wrong rod again. I thought the river would be high and coloured and so took only a spinning rod. It had fallen to almost summer levels and was carrying the slightest stain. I fished through the Meadows with the spinning rod with little hope and less luck.

Walking back to the top of the run I found another fisherman into a fine salmon which had taken his small tube fly. It had taken where I would expect to find a fish and it must have been covered well by my plug only half an hour before.

I do not like carrying an excess of kit but when conditions are marginal like this I should perhaps put another rod in the car!

FISH CAUGHT	0	FLY/LURE	

their lie. Salmon however often follow a fly and take when it is hanging in the stream. A twitch or short pull often helps, but a salmon will take a fly lying static in the current. I have not known a sea trout to take a fly like this.

The sea trout is an impulsive fish. It either attacks or leaves the lure and no amount of teasing or tempting will persuade it to do otherwise. Salmon are not always so fussy. In fact they often need to be pestered and even goaded to show interest in a lure.

Salmon can be provoked several times to rise to a lure and may take on the second, third or even fourth attempt. Resting it for half an hour or so after a missed take and returning can result in success. Jim, one of the old-timers whispered to me one day that "once a salmon has been found it can be caught". By returning again and again and putting different size flies over the fish he was certain that sooner or later the fish would succumb. On a small spate river salmon will take up residency in the small pools and pots and make themselves prone to such tactics. Sea trout will not tolerate any harassment and will seek out cover or run out of the pool if bothered in this way.

Casting over a salmon for long periods is not considering sporting on the rivers I fish and is discouraged. Having had a couple of casts and been refused I tend to move on and give other anglers a chance. But I may return to the location and try again if other pools prove fruitless - and may even return again if there is no one else to try for it.

On the small moorland streams when a salmon rises and follows the fly across a pool it may run out of space before it decides or has had chance to take. This is positive as it shows that the fish is in the right 'mood' and can be caught. As long as it turned away because it had insufficient room to take the lure and not because it was frightened by seeing the angler,

the salmon may be tempted to have another go. It may take some resting and returning to it and some changes in the presentation so that it does have the required 'leg room' but a salmon has an inclination to rise to the fly once can be persuaded to rise again. The point that I am perhaps belabouring is that in this behaviour that it differs most from sea trout.

If the salmon cannot be tempted by recasting once or twice it is sensible to leave the fish to rest and continue to fish the remaining water but then go back to the fish and work down towards the lie again. Start well above where the fish showed and progress towards it carefully, patiently and methodically giving close attention (and an extra cast or two or three) to where the fish was seen. Unless the conditions are enabling fish to run out of the pool there is a good chance that fish may be enticed.

Sometimes a smaller fly will work the magic. If that fails it is often suggested that you put on the biggest fly you have. The big fly has never worked for me but as long as I can remain out of sight, resting and returning to cover the fish as slowly and gently as possible has regularly produced results.

It is sometimes an advantage to be the first one to fish down a beat when fishing for sea trout. Some of my friends who know their water well will be up early after overnight rain to be the first to fish a beat when sea trout are running. It is not necessary to be the first to cover the pools when fishing for salmon. I have done well on a many occasions when following others down a beat. At times it seems positively beneficial to have had the fish warmed up so to speak, by another angler. Especially if they were spinning and I was using a slowly fished fly.

When hooked the salmon and the sea trout will fight very differently. While every fish is different there are patterns and it may help land a fish if this is acknowledged.

DATE	RIVER	BEAT	CONDITIONS
September 1988	Walkham	Upper	Overnight rain – strong but clearing river

NOTES

I was late getting out and thought there may already be rods on my preferred beat I took the car upstream and parked at Ward Bridge. Looking over the bridge while trying to decide whether to go up or down stream I saw a pair of salmon in the tail of the Bridge Pool.

Alas the section immediately below the bridge was not available to me so I climbed down to the upstream section and put a long cast down under the bridge. At the third cast there was immediately a powerful take and an explosion of spray. The fish kited across the current to my right and then back into the mainstream on the left side of the river. It then began to 'back off' shaking its head and using the current. I tried to hold on but the inevitable happened and an empty hook was returned to me – one arm of the treble was straightened out almost entirely. In hindsight I should have give it line and it probably would have swum upstream.

A week later in similar conditions I hooked another salmon in the same location. Perhaps the same fish as it followed the previous pattern. This time I was prepared and dropped the rod and let it have free line. The fish circled the pool and took up a lie right in the centre - under the bridge . I took up the slack and eventually pulled the fish up to my stand. Alas it was a coloured cock fish and was returned.

FISH CAUGHT	I salmon about 7lb.	FLY/LURE	Size 3 gold Mepps

A sea trout once hooked 'goes crazy' and in a burst of energy will do everything it can to rid itself of the hook. It will leap, cartwheel, dive and run and the only thing that can be predicted is that its initial fight is unpredictable. It may run hard upstream for as long as it can, it may run towards the rod or it may back off shaking its head. If it has any slack line it will shake free but if it is fought too hard the hook will pull from the tender mouth of a fresh fish. To hook a sea trout requires skill and patience to land one requires something extra. It is important to keep a sensitive but firm line on the fish. As it tires and the spurts of energy become fewer and shorter the angler can take more control, increase the pressure and net, beach or hand out the fish once it is clearly beaten. I have not had the fortune to hook a very large salmon and have only taken one over ten pounds on my club water but I have found each comparatively easy to fight. Sea trout are a much different kettle of fish and the big ones beat me more often than not.

Early in the season I lose big sea trout because I fight them too hard and the hook hold is lost. I excuse myself by saying I am out of practice and need to get the feel of fighting fish on a light line. I sometimes benefit from a day or so at a put and take fishery in March or April to gain some casting and fish fighting practice. Although the soggy farmed rainbow trout are no match for fresh run sea trout getting the feel for a heavy fish certainly helps.

Too often, after the initial take smaller sea trout will lie on the surface and flap frantically. This is not a good omen but side strain with the rod held low and if possible, below the surface is the best remedy. This will encourage the fish to start swimming again and engage in a 'fair' fight. I cannot recall a salmon ever doing this. Initially they stay deep and only break the surface in short splashes of anger or to leap in the air.

Fish that are hooked on a long line downstream will sometimes back away shaking their heads. Occasionally this happens when my lure is taken by a big sea trout lying at the tail of the pool after dark but it often happens to me with salmon in a summer spate. Salmon are prone to taking a lure 'on the dangle' at the very tail of a pool. At first the take is barely noticeable but having felt the hook the salmon tries to back away into the full flow. Salmon use the current to advantage and when I have been unable to follow downstream and tried to hang on I have been broken or the hooks have pulled out. On one occasion the treble hook of the spoon I was using was straightened by a stubborn autumn salmon that backed off into the rapids below a favourite pool. Perhaps this does not happen in slower streams but it is sometimes a frustration on West Country spate streams

If at all possible I try to keep the line tight while I work my way downstream to get adjacent to the fish. This has resulted in some interesting scrambles around trees and along high steep banks. If the way is barred I usually hang on and hope the hooks hold, or the fish runs into the main section of the pool. The latter option has a poor success rate with sea trout but a hooked salmon will often co-operate and head upstream to deep water if given slack line. When line is recovered the fish is usually still attached and the fight can resume.

Once hooked and the angler is trying to bring it to the shore the salmon reveals other differences in its character. There is often a brief flash of rage when it discovers it is constrained and it will run, shake its head and may leap. After the first dash the fight is mainly a succession of powerful but shorter and predictable runs. Using the current more than a sea trout it will kite across the flows shaking its head. It may leap some more but it may also sit on the bottom and sulk for long periods shaking its head. As it gets tired the salmon may be led around like a dog on a lead and taken to a place where netting or tailing is possible.

DATE	RIVER	BEAT	CONDITIONS
September 2006	Tavy	Abbey	Light rain – but a low clear river 17C

NOTES

The river was disappointingly low and clear. The recent rain had not raised it at all. Many salmon and sea trout were showing throughout the beat. I persevered with the spinning rod I carried but regretted leaving the fly rod at home. The sea trout totally ignored all lures and sat motionless on the bottom. To my surprise one salmon followed and took a red and gold FC. It was a small highly coloured cock fish and was returned but it raised hopes. Half an hour later I had another fish of the same size but fresher in the bag.

In crystal clear water the sea trout showed no interest but two salmon were induced to take.

FISH CAUGHT	2 salmon 5 ½ lb one returned.	FLY/LURE	Red and Gold FC 15gm

DATE	RIVER	BEAT	CONDITIONS
October 2006	Tavy	Middle	Light rain – River low but a good light beery flow

NOTES

The river was up a little and looked in good condition for the fly. I set up the camera on Big Pool to get some photographs of casting. On the third cast across the tail there was a little pluck. Instinctively I struck expecting a small peal but a heavier fish pulled away across the stream. There was none of the rush and leap of a fresh sea trout and I thought I had hooked a mature but stale fish. Eventually I got sight of a bright small salmon that circled the pool until it was tired and could be led to the net. A beautiful fish but quite unspectacular fight.

FISH CAUGHT	1 salmon 5 lb	FLY/LURE	Size 10 Treble Jeanie.

The salmon has a much harder mouth than a sea trout and the hook often takes on a firmer hold as the fight continues. It can subsequently be given slack line or fought hard with less risk of losing a hook hold. Jim, the old-timer who gave me much valued advice recommended striking a salmon, making sure it was hooked and then giving it slack line while moving to a position from where it could be fought and landed with greater convenience. Giving slack line to a sea trout will certainly result in its loss.

Salmon often take my sea trout flies, especially when they are being fished slowly over the lies. The 'Special' that is my night time favourite has taken salmon during day and night. The 'Gold Shoulder'' has proved a surprisingly successful salmon fly in falling spates but if deliberately targeting salmon I tend to change flies. I have more confidence in patterns that were created for the purpose.

I lose very few salmon that take a fly tied on a treble hook. Perhaps it is the harder mouth that makes the single hook skid over the jaw and cling feebly to a sliver of skin. I prefer small simple patterns on low water trebles for my clear stream fishing but have become an advocate of a small copper tube in spates.

But salmon fishing is not my first love and tends to be conducted on Autumn afternoons after some seasonal rain. On such days it is very pleasant to walk by the river with a rod and to enjoy the fresh air, casting here and there to seek out a taking salmon. On such occasions, out of laziness rather than design I am likely to leave the fly rod at home and spin with a spoon or a plug.

A seven centimetre, sinking plug has proved excellent lure for salmon fishing on the Tavy. It has the right weight for easy casting and sinks to an appropriate depth to cover most lies effectively. I remove the middle treble in line with my club requirements and sometimes replace the tail hook with one that is stronger. Black and silver is my preferred colour and I will fish down a pool in a series of successive sweeps that allow the lure to cross fish as slowly as possible. I try to slow up its progress to allow it to dangle and tremble over known lies. Deeper gullies may be plumbed with a Mepps type spoon – perhaps casting upstream, allowing the spoon to sink and flutter down to a position level with me so that when retrieved the spoon rises through the water hopefully in front of salmon inducing a take. In recent years I have begun to favour the 'Flying C' for such an approach as these are cheap. I can risk losing them by fishing slow and close the bottom as the spinning rubber tails reduce the chances of getting caught up on the bottom or foul hooking fish.

In heavy water these tactics work for sea trout but are never productive when the visibility exceeds the fishes strike range. Salmon however will take in clear water as long as they have not seen the fisherman. Long casts, or short casts from cover, will tempt salmon to chase and take a lure even in a crystal river. Fish which have been leaping or showing on the surface seem especially vulnerable. As the season progresses they seem to get territorial and may feel the need to chase off small predators which have intentions on their eggs and progeny.

Before all the rods are taken down, put into their bags and hung up in the cupboard for the winter it is gratifying to have taken a salmon or two. I enjoy the late summer and autumn fishing but when I reflect upon the season it is the sea trout that are always the most memorable. As I hang up the rods I look forward to the Spring and the coming of the bluebells when the peal will be running the rivers once again.

Chapter 9

The Limit

It is estimated that ur species, homo sapiens first appeared in the highlands of East Africa some 200,000 years ago. On the African Plains our ancestors were omnivorous and existed as 'scavengers', or perhaps more romantically, as 'hunter-gatherers'. The population spread around the Indian Ocean then into the Mediterranean and East Asia 50, 000 - 60,000 years ago. About 11,000 – 13,000 years ago farming began in Syria and from then our modern lifestyles evolved. As we developed as 'hunter-gatherers', our bodies and our social relationships evolved to be effective at finding, collecting and catching food as well as existing in a wild untamed world. Our capacity for thought and planning and our emotions developed to make us efficient and successful in this respect.

When we became farmers we developed a very different lifestyle. We remained in fixed settlements and hunting and scavenging became less and less important to our existence. We moved into settled communities and lived by farming, trade and very recently manufacture. In terms of the total time humans have lived on earth this is a relatively short period - just 5-6% of our existence as a species. There are many of our species, around the globe, that continue to exist just as our early ancestors did. They have never needed to make the change to a 'western lifestyle' and continue to live as hunter gatherers.

It would be surprising indeed if we were able to shake off the psychological attributes that made our species successful for 95% of our time on this planet. It is likely that we still have deep within us emotional drives that come from our ancestral background. That we still need to express these emotions through engaging in hunting and gathering is perhaps predictable. Research into addiction and cravings have identified a chemical transmitter (dopamine) that is released by the brain when we engage in activities that are essential to our survival. This gives pleasure, rewards us and encourages us to continue with these activities. The neuroscientists cite eating, drinking and sex as prime examples of type of action that can trigger a dopamine release but the researchers believe that the list extends beyond these basic impulses. Shelter building, clothing, tool making, hunting and fishing have been important to our survival for thousands of years and it is thought that these activities continue to give us pleasure because they stimulate the same dopamine release as eating, drinking and sex!

In the modern world few of us choose to obtain our food through foraging - it is hard and uncertain work. We choose to work in manufacturing or service industries, living in ways that bare very little comparison to those of our not-so-distant predecessors. Much of our food come pre-packed, washed and trimmed by the supermarket complete with multiple 'air-miles'. It is convenience food that serves a purpose but sometimes leaves us a little unsatisfied.

We have not had to hunt down, kill, prepare or cook it - activities central to our lives for thousands of years. It is of little surprise that we often find our lives are missing something. Our working days do not produce the dopamine release that our ancestors enjoyed while ensuring their survival. Some of us need to use our 'leisure time' to re-engage with those activities that create a more deep-seated sense of satisfaction.

DATE	RIVER	BEAT	CONDITIONS
July 2005	Tavy	Middle	Low clear 17C

NOTES

I was tempted to stay in, sit and watch television, go to bed with a book and take up a whiskey. But I knew that the events of the day would be running over in my mind and I would be wrestling with a solution to the latest problem that work had thrown up until it was time to get up and go in to face it. At 9.00 I needed some fishing. The river was low and very clear and although the bats were flying I could still see stones on riverbed and I needed to wait for dark before starting. While the sun went down and the moon came up the air was 'heady' with the scent of honeysuckle and a family of owls began calling to each other across the river, a badger grunted along the footpath behind me and a roe deer ran across a clearing in the wood opposite.

Old Jim, another fisherman arrived and after a brief exchange of notes we agreed starting places and once all colours were washed from the valley we began to fish. For over two hours I worked my way slowly through the darkness trying to make each cast right. There was no exertion, no stretching, I worked with a steady rhythm focusing on placing my flies with gentle precision. The rhythm was only broken by rising fish and the short battles to control and land those that were hooked. My companion continued likewise and we did not speak until both had finished. We exchanged notes and recounted where fish had been found and where fish had been lost. We compared catches (he had done better) and we left for home.

The problem at work was forgotten until I arrived at my desk the next day. The solution was then quite obvious

FISH CAUGHT	4 sea trout all 1lb	FLY/LURE	Half silver Size 10

DATE	RIVER	BEAT	CONDITIONS
July 2005	Tavy	Lower	Low and clear 18C – 15C

NOTES

Fished the Run and took what I thought was a small peal on a Half Silver point fly. I did not want to wade ashore and so unhooked it in the net and dropped it in the bag. Two metres on I took another on the dropper. When I got home I found that one of the fish was a brown trout identical in size to the peal. The brown was full of small snails.
It was cleaned and eaten but its fleah was bland and if anything a little muddy tasting. I regretted taking it - even if it was a mistake. The sea trout was pink and delicate in flavour - with just a hint of the sea remaining.. I should have spotted the difference when I lifted the fish out of the net. Brown trout always feel much softer.

FISH CAUGHT	1 sea trout 12oz 1 brown trout 12oz	FLY/LURE	Size 10s - Half silver and blue special.

DATE	RIVER	BEAT	CONDITIONS
October 2003	Tavy	Middle	Falling spate - clearing

NOTES

Not long after starting to fish I hooked a large and beautifully coloured cock salmon (on a tube fly) in 'The Run'. It put up an unspectacular but long and determined fight and proved very difficult to get near the net. Its size, the strength of current and the position made a swift grassing impossible. Eventually I let it take me down to the pool and beached it on the gravel. The treble hook was lodged at the back of the mouth and challenged my forceps to get it ot.. When I did eventually remove the hook the tired fish seemed to have given up the ghost. I held it back in the stream until my arm ached and although its was still breathing it would not take over control and swim away. Each time I let it go it rolled over on its back and allowed itself to be washed away. Each time I retrieved it from the where it washed up in the shallows and tried again.

I did not want to kill and take the fish as it was clearly not fit to eat and was getting despondent. Eventually I wedged the fish upright between some large pebbles in the neck of the pool and went back to fish the run.

Half an hour later as I worked my way down towards the pool I heard a great deal of splashing. I dropped my rod and hurried down to see what was happening. The salmon left for dead had come to life and was thrashing in the shallows. I shepherded it towards deeper water where it was clearly able to hold position in the stream. It leapt and I never saw it again. Some three hours later I returned to see if it had succumbed and washed up in the tail but there was no sign

FISH CAUGHT	1 Salmon 8lb(?) returned	FLY/LURE	1'' Blue and pearl tube

DATE	RIVER	BEAT	CONDITIONS
July 2005	Tavy	Lower	Dark peat stained water with a little sediment but no debris 18C

NOTES

Arrived at the river early after a day and night of intermittent rain. Tracks suggested I was not the first but I fished through the meadows with a fly rod. I took two good 'schoolies' in the first run and then sat in the long grasses watching a heron who seemed to be enjoying less luck than me. I left for home having thoroughly enjoyed the few hours hour and got home for breakfast.

I subsequently met the Label, another fisherman who had fished that morning. Having seen my car he dashed downstream to get ahead of me and fished frantically until early afternoon with a spinning rod. He claimed to have landed 16 sea trout taking 4 but somehow I think I had enjoyed the day more!

FISH CAUGHT	2 sea trout 1lb 4 oz, 1lb 1oz	FLY/LURE	Size 10 Bead head

We follow sports that give us an excuse for clan bonding and symbolised tribal warfare. (We now kick balls at the opposition rather than attack them with arrows and spears.) Shopping has taken the place of scavenging and we have turned shelter building into DIY. When night falls we come together in our living rooms to receive stories from the television rather than tell tales around the campfire. Modern life has brought safety, security and freedom from famine but it has robbed us of opportunities to express many of our deep-seated drives. The feel good factors that were dripped into our systems by hunter-gatherer lifestyles are missing and may be the cause of misery, distress and reliance on chemical stimulants for many.

We need opportunities to connect with our inner selves, the self that needs to journey and explore wild places. The self that needs to plan, prepare, develop strategies and exercise strength and skill. These are very basic and primitive needs that may well be dormant in many of us but in others the need gnaws at us, makes us edgy and restless until we find a resolution.

For most of the working week we can play the part of modern man and nine to five switch off our primitive selves to dutifully attend to our daily tasks. But once work has finished and we have been fed and fuelled we are ready to return to less civilised ways. Media and publishing help many to self-actualisation by creating opportunities to live their primitive lives by proxy. Using our imagination and inspired by the stories of others we travel, explore, adventure, do battle and hunt from our armchairs. But some of us still need the physical involvement with an activity that is built into our make up– some us need to go fishing!

Without over-romanticising the concept, our ancestors almost certainly had some affinity with the land. They would have understood the seasons and known when to gather berries,

pick nuts, trap fowl and net fish. They had a vested interest in the continuation of the harvests from one year to another and would not take more than they had need of. Without this they would not have survived. There was no place for waste or greed as these would be self-defeating. Somehow we find it difficult to reconnect with this and it is sometimes difficult to exercise restraint having become detached from a culture that relied upon it.

Conservation is necessary. Populations are growing and land shrinking with true wild life limited to few precious contracting areas. The fish that run our rivers have been extremely hard hit and we cannot crop and crop and expect to carry on doing so. Although it conflicts with the integral spirit of freedom in fishing we must accept some control if we want to be able to have fish to catch. A responsible sense of custodianship is necessary.

'Catch and release' has always been part of my fishing. I have always targeted specific, edible species and always returned undersized fish and unwanted species. There is an inevitable 'by-catch' and I deal with it as humanely and responsibly as I can. The small fry, smolts and small brown trout that I often catch when seeking out larger fish are easily shaken off a single hook with little lasting damage. At times they can be a welcome diversion to an otherwise quiet period but usually they are a hindrance and I regret causing them distress or damage.

Despite being often tempted to cast to small rising fish on a blank day I now try to avoid them. For similar reasons I avoid fishing the lower river early in the year when salmon kelts are likely to be present and do not fish for salmon over the late autumn gravel runs when gravid sea trout will be assembling to spawn.

DATE	RIVER	BEAT	CONDITIONS
July 2003	Tavy	Middle	Low and clear 18C – 15C

NOTES

Arrived at the pool to find Derek in place and about to start. Nothing moved until quite late when I found a shoal. I then quickly had a brace and stopped to exchange notes. The other angler had not had a touch and seemed despondent so we exchanged positions. I was going to leave but to encourage him I fished on and succeeded in taking another brace from his stand. I then joined him to see how he had progressed. Still nothing!.. and the spirit was waning so I did not confess to my second brace. To help, I demonstrated where I had cast and found fish and was immediately into yet another peal. At this stage I just had to stop and stood by directing until he was finally into a fish. I then left him to it. He subsequently took another two including a fish of 3lb and phoned the next day to claim he had 'beaten me'. I congratulated him and did not reveal the true size of my bag that night.

FISH CAUGHT	5 sea trout 2lb 1oz, 2lb, 1lb 8oz, 1lb 12 oz, 1lb.	FLY/LURE	Size 10s - Half Silver and Black Special.

DATE	RIVER	BEAT	CONDITIONS
August 2002	Tavy	Lower	Very Light but no direct moonlight, 16C

NOTES

Took two small peal from the Run and a pug fish of 4lb+. I put the latter under the torch and found it was lightly hooked. It was also darkly spotted and beginning to feel soft in strong contrast to the firm fresh fish. It was not going to make good eating and I was near my limit and so I returned it unharmed. Looking at my diaries it was my best fish of the season but I was glad it had been returned. The peal were delicious.

FISH CAUGHT	2 sea trout 4lb 12oz, 10oz.	FLY/LURE	Size 10 Black and Orange Special

DATE	RIVER	BEAT	CONDITIONS
September 1989	Walkham	Magpie	River up after rain. Peat stained with some sediment

NOTES

Fished down the Magpie stretch in perfect conditions but had no luck Half way down I passed two visiting anglers who had no luck and were grumbling about another pair of fishermen who had been using 'natural' bait. Having fished all through the beat with no success I met a third 'angler' at Grenofen Bridge who boasted of taking two salmon.

He was very reluctant to show me the fish but when I showed some scepticism he opened his car boot to reveal a fine bright cock fish of about 9lb. As fine a fish as I have seen come from that beat. Alongside was a dark coloured hen fish that was clearly 'unclean'. I admitted envy at the silver fish but asked why the hen had been killed? It had taken the worm down was the reply!

FISH CAUGHT	0	FLY/LURE	CD7 S

Frequently I catch brown trout when fishing for their migratory cousins and at times it is impossible to avoid hooking more than the odd one. Giving slack line often allows them to shake themselves free but most often they must be landed and unhooked. There was a time when I would take large brown trout, in the belief that they were cannibalistic and were better out of the river. Any damage they do to juvenile fish is probably countered by their potential to spawn many more. In my early days as a sea trout fisherman a few were inadvertently 'bagged' in mistake for a peal when fishing at night and before I developed my sense of touch. When I reach into the net for a fish that is of a pound or less and it feels a little soft I now unhook it swiftly and return without any further damage. If the fish is larger and it yields in my grasp as I take it from the net I may put a light on it – really out of curiosity more than to check but sea trout make better eating and so I return all brown trout.

I also return late season sea trout, caught when salmon fishing and any 'coloured' and gravid salmon (this is required by law). Catching and returning fish that are caught incidentally causes me no concern. I have some difficulty however, with deliberately pursuing fish that I am going to submit to some, however small, trauma only to release, once my fun with them is finished. On rare occasions, I join friends for some coarse fishing during the trout close season and when 'withdrawal symptoms' have got the better of me. Coarse fish do seem to cope extremely well with being caught and released again and again and I am sure that it does no permanent harm but it is not really 'my bag'. I think there is purity in hunting 'fish for the table'. A fish or two gives me a sufficient dopamine rush and I stop fishing with satisfaction once and if I have caught enough for a meal.

For some years I thought that catching salmonoids with the intention of returning them was irresponsible. I thought that many of these fish would not survive to spawn and that treating them like coarse fish was entirely wrong. But I have learnt from the experiences of those who have been catching fish for egg collection schemes. It seems that salmon are more resilient than I thought and they are capable of surviving to spawn despite the trauma of capture. If handled carefully! There have been times when a salmon has been particularly difficult to land from high bank and has been forced to endure more stress while a deep hook was removed. Such fish have been returned to the river with few signs of life just the vestiges of breathing in the slowly pulsing gills. I had little hope of their survival and on more than one occasion gave up hope as the fish rolled over on its back and floated away. I have since discovered that persistence will repay you and a tired fish that is to be returned will survive if held upright and into the stream. It will sooner or later recover but it may take some time.

There was a time when I thought that the best fishermen on the river were those who amassed the largest tally of fish in a season. I stood in awe of those who casually sent in returns of fifty or a hundred sea trout and I wanted to emulate them. I wanted to be up there amongst them and become an even 'better' fisherman! I was determined to challenge the 'top rod' on the river.

Eventually I reached the 'half-century' and in addition caught five salmon. This was more than I, and my family really wanted to consume and my wife would groan when I returned with yet another 'good catch'. I gave some to friends, had some smoked and froze a lot, but could not cope with as much fish. My fishing was for pleasure, but dealing with the volume of fish I was catching was diminishing my enjoyment. Competition had got the better of me and I was ultimately poorer for it. It took a whole season but I saw sense and realised that my 'success' had not made me a 'good fisherman'. I wanted

to continue to enjoy the pleasures of fishing but did not need so much fish.

Fish can be sold, and there is a market for sea trout but my fishing permit forbids the sale of fish caught on the club waters. I have always had an aversion to selling sea trout and selling a catch would put my fishing on a very different footing. Taking fish that I did not personally need, to sell, would be greedily depriving others of the chance of catching the fish and it would it be selfish and disrespectful. I enjoy having a few extra to give those I know enjoy the occasional treat but accept nothing in return. Sharing ones bounty is part of the joy of the sport.

For those who want to be competitive there are other ways of doing so without amassing dead bodies. When the rule forbidding the sale of wild fish was introduced the old boys in my club would compete to see who could be the first to land a sea trout after the opening of the season. Getting a fish by St Patrick's Day was the goal! Others set out to make things equally difficult by fishing with vintage tackle or methods that demanded high levels of skill. This is much more sporting and is to be applauded.

I now approach my fishing with a personal and somewhat flexible bag limit. On most nights (or days) I am very happy to take a brace of fish - one fish can be caught almost accidentally but two fish proves it was no fluke (perhaps). During lean periods, when time to fish or indeed luck has been in short supply I may continue after taking a brace and if my fortune holds take another one or two fish. But generally I am content to take a peal or two, walk the beat and leave much of the river untouched for others to try.

With a brace of fresh sea trout in the bag I am a very happy man and on warm night or sunny day I am content to stop fishing and sit, listen to the wildlife and watch the river. If there is anyone else fishing who has not enjoyed such

good luck and who can be subjected to my advice 'my cup runneth over'!

Over recent seasons I have limited myself to no more than thirty sea trout and perhaps a salmon or two. This is sufficient to enjoy through the summer, keep friends and family happy and have one or two to freeze for the occasional winter treat. Fresh run sea trout are the most enjoyable fish to catch and to eat. They are a summer luxury unsurpassed by any other fare and are delicious when baked in foil, poached in wine or quickly grilled. I have experimented with many different recipes but the delicate flavour is lost when combined with any strong spices or herbs. Sea trout are best lightly cooked and presented simply.

The finest fish to eat are the early run 'maiden peal'. Fish that have had a full winter at sea and are returning to the river for the first time. These vary in weight from just under 1 kilo to just under 2 kilos and begin to appear in April and continue to June. In July and August these are spreading through the river and are difficult to locate. These are fish that have enjoyed the maximum time at sea and are full of fats and oils that are going to sustain them until spawning in late October. In May or June before eggs or milt have developed there is not a better fish for the table, their flesh is rose pink and melts in the mouth. I do not catch so many of these fish that I can afford to return that many.

As the run of 'maiden peal' begins to 'peter out' they are replaced in July and August by the 'harvest or school peal', small bright fish up to half a kilogram in weight. Some of these may not mature sexually and will return to sea without spawning. 'Schoolies' provide good sport during late summer and make excellent eating through to the end of the season. I have no hesitation in keeping a brace of the larger ones for the table up to the very end of August while I return mature sea trout (over 1 kilogram) during the latter months of the season.

Mature fish begin to lose their silver sheen in September and take on warmer hues, seeming to gain even more spots to merge with the spawning gravels. They lose some of their reserve and at times can be aggressive and easily caught. The Welsh 'sewin' anglers call these fish 'dalen twp' or sometimes the Anglicised version 'twps y dail'. Literally translated this means 'stupid leaves' and the term expresses the autumn colour and behaviour of the ripe fish.

'Pug" fish as they were known on the Torridge where I grew up, are sea trout that have spawned previously and are returning for their second, third or so spawning season. They tend to be large and heavily spotted. Male fish develop a 'kype' and can become ugly brutes. They will make good eating in the early months of the season but once August has arrived they are beginning to fill with eggs or milt and the quality of the flesh deteriorates. All late caught mature fish are past their culinary best and I prefer to return them. Many fishing associations ban the taking of sea trout in September although they can be legally killed through to end of the month. I now stop targeting sea trout once August is past or earlier if I have been blessed and have already had my fill.

I could continue and 'catch and release' but I tend not to do this. It is, in part that I am not happy causing unnecessary stress or damage to a fish I have no intention of keeping. If I have been fortunate enough to catch enough for my needs I stop fishing and may 'walk the water', enjoy the environment or chat with other fishermen. Continuing to 'catch and release' would only serve to add to a pointless tally. I now know that fish handled carefully can be released with little impact on their chances of survival but a sea trout caught and released is very unlikely to be caught again during that season. There are others who share my fishing and it would be greedy to spoil their chances of success. Fish, we now know, have memories and I do not believe a returned sea trout will be caught again that season. While I understand the motives behind the concept that a sea trout is too good to be caught once I don't think any are ever caught twice. I therefore restrict my 'catch and release' to those undersize or stale fish that are inadvertently hooked. My club asks that hen salmon are returned and these also go back to spawn as do 'stale' sea trout. Clean fish are taken until I reach my limit and then I stop.

Readers who have read so far may have noticed that I have not mentioned fishing with the worm or any other live bait. An opinion may have developed that I have no knowledge of this method of fishing or side with those who are 'anti worming'. The main reason for my omission is that my fishing association forbids the use of 'natural bait' and I have subsequently focused on the use of artificial lures. This has given me sufficient fish over the years and I have rarely felt it necessary to use any other methods. While I will happily use rag worms, sand eels and mackerel strip when sea fishing I seem to have an inbuilt reluctance to use bait in fresh water. I have some friends who are violently opposed to the use of the worm for fishing for trout and salmon and other friends who commend it. Most anglers begin fishing with a worm and in this respect I am no exception. I too began angling as a small boy with a worm and a bent pin. Although I now have access to fishing where worming is permitted I have not been at all tempted to go back to my childhood in this respect. I prefer to apply other methods.

I like to be active when fishing, I like the physical activity of casting a fly and lure and working my way up or down a stream. I enjoy deceiving a fish on a fly or lure that I have devised and made myself. Putting up the deck chair, impaling a little wriggler, casting out and waiting for a bite is not as enjoyable - it is not the same aesthetic experience. Also, I can during most seasons achieve my limit with the methods I

DATE	RIVER	BEAT	CONDITIONS
January 2003			

NOTES

At the Fishing Club AGM someone carrying out research into 'why people go fishing' had written in to the secretary. They were seeking subjects for the study and asked for comments. There was a brief silence while the collective anus clanched in preparation for a release of romantic twaddle. Fortunately someone at the back got in first and called out 'Because I like to kill them!' There was relieved laughter and we moved on to the next item.

FISH CAUGHT		FLY/LURE	

find more interesting and challenging. Worming may produce an easy fish or two but for me (with a limit) it may produce too many fish too soon. But when age finally gets a grip on me I may be content to be wheeled out to sit by the weir pool and drown a worm or two This form of fishing does give a great deal of pleasure to those whose skills or mobility is challenged and it would be sad if it were not permitted, but while I can still walk the banks I will continue to fish the artificial fly.

I am also concerned that fishing natural baits and the worm in particular is not entirely compatible with the fish's welfare. I have stopped fishing upstream with small spinners as this seemed to attract a disproportionate number of immature fish that were often difficult to remove from the treble hook without causing significant damage. A fish that swallows a worm and a hook is pretty much a dead fish no matter how big or small. I used to believe that hooks taken down to deep to be easily disgorged were better left to the fish's digestive juices to deal with. The theory was that normal steel hooks would be dissolved. This alas, does not seem to be the case.

Salmon kept in captivity to harvest eggs and milt for West Country restocking schemes have shown remarkable resilience. They survive well until spawning time arrives and are able to be released alive after stripping. This adds to the evidence that disproves my early theory that a fish subjected to capture on rod and line would be stressed so much that its survival was unlikely. Some fish have died while being kept and autopsies have been carried out to establish the cause. All the fish that died were found to have hooks in their gut having completely swallowed a natural bait. Fish that died within 48 hours of capture always contained a hook that had torn the gut and an internal organ had been pierced. If the gut was merely pierced by the hook the fish, was found to survive for up to a month but by this time septicaemia

would overcome it. Possibly a hook in the gut of a non-migratory fish with an active stomach would not have the same result but it is clearly deadly to salmon. Although I have no proof, I see no reason why sea trout should be any different. These facts are now well known but many worm fishermen are reluctant to accept it.

Clearly leaving a hook in the gut of a salmon or a sea trout is quite unacceptable and this knowledge has made me feel even more uncomfortable about bait fishing. These are critical issues of animal welfare that could spoil my plans for retirement by the weir, with my rug over my knees - but I may have an answer.

There is a revival in interest in the 'circle hook'. This ancient form of hook has been brought back into use by commercial long line fishermen. The attraction of the circle hook is that it does take quite an exceptional hold in the 'scissors' of a fish's jaw but if swallowed the hook can be pulled back through the gut without catching - until it reaches the fish's mouth it is pulled around to hook firmly in the corner of the gape. The traditional 'J' hook is designed to gain a hold wherever it can and this is as likely to be in the throat or the stomach as the jaw. Apart form the welfare issue the circle hook does provide a much more secure hold and its devotees report a much higher strike to landing ratio. I am informed that it is best not to strike but to tighten as the fish moves away.

I am hoping that it may not come to it, but if I do become physically unable to fish with more active methods I may have to resort to bait fishing. If I do I will be using circle hooks but in the meantime I will continue to enjoy fishing with a fly. This give me all the sport I require with no lasting damage to the fish I need to return.

Chapter 10
The Stirjin

There was a phrase oft used amongst the fishermen of Appledore as I was growing up. It is one that I have not heard for some years, but from time to time it is a phrase that comes back to me and inwardly I muse 'that was a Stirjin!'

It was a phrase not infrequently heard in the Coach and Horses, the Royal George, Royal Hotel, Seagate, Beaver, Prince of Wales, Rising Sun, Bell Inn, Globe or one of the many public houses that then existed at that time as fishermen, sailors and shipwrights told stories and relived adventures. In the 1950s I was regularly smuggled into one or other by my Grandfather, and made to sit in a corner with a bottle of pop and a packet of crisps while he enjoyed a lunchtime glass. It was here, or in the galley on the Roma the steamship that he still skippered, that I probably first heard the phrase. I also heard it on the Quay as fishermen hauled kit and catch from their boats below. 'But a Stirjin!' or 'Twas a Stirjin Day! would be called out or sighed with combined relief and happiness.' As a youngster I lapsed into using it before I really knew what it meant and probably misused it as often as not.

The phrase I spilled out when the situation seemed right but I initially had no idea what I was saying. Beyond reading and arithmetic I remember very little being explained to me and I feel I was expected to absorb information and knowledge by some form of osmosis. I was admonished when I got something wrong but had to learn by listening and watching. Once out of nappies I was taken everywhere by my Grandfather and between the bars and cabins of steamers and ketches I picked up enough to get by. I was able to converse effectively in the vernacular, box the compass and set a course for the Bell Buoy before I went to primary school.

Upon progressing to school in Bideford I was thrust into the company of the sons of shop managers, bankers, teachers and policemen. They seemed to speak a different language and quickly I had to adapt. Often my grammatical errors were exposed and ridiculed and I was asked to explain the phrases I was prone to utter. At times this gave me some difficulty and 'Stirgin' really challenged me. It was one of many phrases in the local dialect that had evolved from a long lost source and was not comprehendible to anyone outside the community. In order to explain myself I tried to uncover the origins of the saying and eventually I discovered the source. The phrase arises from one of those classic folk tales of reversed fortunes. The story has several versions with various sub plots and elaborations. To my knowledge it has never been written down and as with other oral histories each teller adds his or her variations and decorations. The version that I recount here is little more than a synopsis but it captures the moral of the tale and explains the roots of my philosophy.

I doubt that the story I recount is true for it has a parallel in almost every fishing port in the West Country. Probably the most famous legend with a similar plot is the tale of the Mousehole Feast and Tom Ballcock's Eve. As with of all of these sagas, what matters is not so much the historical accuracy but the meaning it carries. I have special affection for this version for not only is it set in my place of birth, it illustrates the social climate in which I grew up. Although I have not voiced it in many years

'Stirgin' has given me a way to express a deep fulfilment.

The story, like many similar tales, recounts hard times with heavy weather keeping the boats in port. Eventually the clouds opened and the sun shone down and the wide and dangerous estuary became calm and peaceful once again. As the tide ebbed the salmon fishing boats left for the distant sandbanks. It was a beautiful day and all the boats had some success and returned safely to a relieved village in triumph. The last boat to return had, in addition to a few salmon had a huge fish in tow. It had been taken in the net and heaved ashore where it was despatched without hesitation. When the tide flooded the bank from which they were fishing, the four-man crew could not lift the large fish into the boat and so they towed it home. Back in port it was raised by a boat-lifting derrick on one of the quays and put onto a cart.

No one new what the fish was – at first it was thought to be a shark but it did not have the teeth or the skin of such an animal. The mystery was cleared up when the agent arrived to buy the salmon. It was declared to be a sturgeon and as such it had to be offered to the King. The crew of the boat was resigned to having their prize taken from them and a message was sent to London. In the village the threat of famine had retreated and when word from the capital was returned – the King had had declined to accept the fish. So the agent returned and the sturgeon was sold for a 'vast sum'.

The boat's owner and potentially the major benefactor, persuaded the crew to take the proceeds and give them to the poor of the village. "Us is fit and us can work and the good Lord has given us an end to the gales. Now we have had a day when bending the back to the oars and hauling the net was a pleasure beyond all pleasures. We have been given a great fish that was taken from us and then given back once more. It is right that we should give him

up once again to help those who cannot work and to give thanks for that beautiful day – that Stirjin Day".

I left Appledore in the 1960s and have not heard the phrase since. I return regularly, to see family and may take a glass in one of the village pubs or loiter by the Seagate steps to watch the fishing boats but things have changed and I have not heard mention of a 'Stirjin' in any location. Undoubtedly there is some old salt propped up in a chair in some residential home reminiscing about 'Stirjin Days' to the confusion of his carers. One day it may happen to me too. I still recall bright blue days standing on the slip and watching the boats come in on the flood. I remember watching a fisherman clumping up the steps meeting enquiries as to his luck by lifting a modest catch and returning with 'but a Stirjin!' The word became used to sum up a good day when honest labour was rewarded with an adequate material return but the greater prize was a spiritual gain. I once heard it used to celebrate a birth! "Av ee got a boy or a maid? Tommy" was called across Market Street. "I got a Stirjin" beamed back the proud father.

Many years on and living a different life I still enjoy days when the beauty of the world seems to overwhelm me and I think it's a 'Stirjin Day'. A good day in the garden or a long walk over the moors creates a similar feeling but it is when fishing that I feel that sense of pleasure that really makes me recall that phrase from my youth. It is not the catch of a great number or great size of fish but time spent in honest exercise in bright clean air and sparkling water.

Catching a fish, is the prime intention of the activity, and the deception of sea trout has become an obsession but in truth the prize is not always the one that fills my bag. I enjoy many 'fruitless' visits to the river, especially early in the season. Fish are few and far between and although in prime condition and the most challenging they are not encountered that often.

DATE	RIVER	BEAT	CONDITIONS
April 2006	Walkham	Upper	

NOTES
Sections of the upper Walkham had become overgrown and too difficult to fish and so we had a working party to clear some of the bank and introduce new members to some under-fished beats. The morning was bright and crisp and although cold at first we were soon stripping off the layers. The sun was shining the birds were singing and the first leaves were bursting. We were exhausted but happy – a Stirjin!

FISH CAUGHT		FLY/LURE	

DATE	RIVER	BEAT	CONDITIONS
May 2004	Tavy	Middle	14C Low clear

NOTES
The first warm night of the year and I drove to the river past high lush banks speckled with bluebells and campions. Across the moor the first of the pony foals was gambolling around its mother in the evening sunshine and as I descended into the valley the bursting oaks were full of singing birds and the breeze carried an air of wild garlic. As darkness descended the bats replaced the birds and there were great splashes in the pool as fish announced their presence. I began fishing when I could no longer read my watch and before long had hooked three brown trout and one smolt. All returned. The huge sea trout that were cartwheeling around the pool were evading me but eventually I had a solid tug and a good fish was on. It bore down, leapt in the air and then thrashed on the surface. Putting the rod tip under the water failed to get it swimming again and it threw the hook. I fished on but could not raise another and left about midnight happy that I had deceived and hooked a fish.
It was a good first night of the season – a Stirjin'

FISH CAUGHT	3 browns 1 smolt	FLY/LURE	Silver special 8

DATE	RIVER	BEAT	CONDITIONS
May 2000	Tavy	Middle	Low and clear

NOTES
I was joined by two friends and fellow club members to fish for sea trout. Throughout the night their conversation and banter was entertaining and I went home with my face aching from laughing so much. But we did very little real fishing - it proved difficult to retain any sense of the surroundings and we all got into tangles and subsequently we all left fishless. A very pleasant night but perhaps we should have all gone to the pub instead.

FISH CAUGHT	0	FLY/LURE	

Although I set out with hopes of hooking one of these I am happy just to reacquaint myself with the river, watch the wildlife and begin to plan the season.

Throughout the close season, when it is forbidden to fish, I take occasional walks by the river. In part just for the pleasure of walking by running water. It provides opportunity to look at the way the floods have changed the riverbed and look forward to the next year's fishing. Without the cloak of summer foliage the river valley is exposed and I can view sections of the river that are denied to me for much of the fishing season.

I look at places where fish have been caught or lost and take advantage of the bare branches to look into places that all summer have been hidden. In January when the river level is restrained by frost on the moor every pebble can be seen through the crystal steams. In reality it is fishing that has brought me to the river even when I cannot fish. In part it is preparation for the next season, in part a review of the last one but mainly it is to dream. If I could not fish I would continue to visit the river for the pure enjoyment of it but with much less frequency. I would not visit it several times a week during the fishing season nor give up four or more days a year to work on its banks when the season is yet to get under way.

Early season fish are large but scarce. They are often encountered but rarely landed and my earliest sea trout has come to my net on the 9th of April. On most years I do not land a sea trout until May. The nights in April tend to be too cold for fishing with a floating line and it is hard to locate fish in the spring spates but it is hard to hold back once the season has officially begun. As soon as I have some free time and there is colour in the water I am out exploring the changes made to the river by the winter floods. I rarely catch a fish but there is always the possibility of a large fresh sea trout or a

tussle with one. Opportunities I find are hard to let pass. A day by the river in early spring with wild daffodils and bird song is a day to enjoy and with a fish or not there is fresh knowledge to be carried home. This is perhaps the 'Stirjin' that can make such a day so rewarding.

Before the serious matter of night fishing gets under way, the club organises working parties to pull out any dead trees or debris washed down during the close season and trim the banks here and there to create some room to cast and some ease of access. In the spring sunshine this is enjoyable work and at the end of a hard morning when the muscles are a little stiff after a lazy winter but a job has been well done there is a sense of satisfaction and I get that 'Stirjin' feeling.

In May the beech leaves have just opened and in the sunlight their bright transparent green gives the world a fresh optimistic glow. The blackthorn comes into flower and the campions and bluebells herald the first sea trout. I drive to the river through sunny canyons of wild flowers, in hope of a bright fresh fish but happy just to be out in the fresh air.

Fishing in itself is a deeply meditative activity. It cannot be rushed and the successful sea trout fisherman is the one that works, quietly, carefully and methodically. This comes hard for me for my days have been filled with activity, rushing and constant urgency. At times I am still mentally speeding when I hit the river, but once focused I soon settle down. I never entirely relax but switching my mind and body into a different mode is somehow more relaxing. I sit and plan my night and unless another fisherman appears and has to be accommodated I stick to my strategy. It usually involves starting at the top of the section I intend to fish and working down and casting in a gentle steady rhythm. I try to reach the hot spots, into a calm and comfortable tempo, fishing well and timing my arrival to coincide with total darkness. Taking

time out to engage with the slow steady rhythm of the river has undoubtedly been good for me. It has allowed me to regain some equilibrium, to reset my perspective and approach daily life with a little renewed vigour. The Chinese (I think) have a proverb that goes something like 'days spent fishing are not counted towards a man's lifespan'. It's a nice idea!

On those nights when I find it difficult to sleep – when the day has been full of unresolved problems that I have brought home and take to bed with a racing mind I would like to get up and pop down to the river. Alas this is rarely possible but I can do so in my mind. As I lie awake I try to picture myself fishing down a favourite stretch. I step into the water above the neck of the pool and imagine the water trickling around my ankles. It is late May or June and with sunlight breaking on fresh leaves the stream runs through an untroubled valley. Feeling a gentle breeze on my face I roll out an easy cast and lengthen line until the flies are sweeping the narrow channel at the top of the pool. I wave the rod tip this way and that watching the line and envisaging the lures fluttering in the current. Gradually I move down and lengthen the line to cover the body of the pool with longer but easy casts and watch each one sweep the boulders and gullies where fish like to lie. I 'fish out' each cast at the water's pace and lift the line smoothly to recast in unhurried rhythms. Before I reach the tail I am invariably asleep and before I've caught a fish.

From time to time I meet a man who walks a mile or so from where he can park his car to one of the old fishing shelters on the Tavy. Here he sits to watch the river and while enjoying the peace and tranquillity he writes poetry and short stories. From time to time I blunder into his peace and disturb his solitude. I stop and make polite conversation and we tell of what each other has seen and heard. Like me he has developed a great love of the river and the life it shows us. We have this in common but while

he journeys to the river to enjoy it for its own sake and while he is there he engages in his diversion, I journey to the river to engage in my quest and while there enjoy its beauty.

The fish have drawn me to the river and in my efforts to find and entice them I have become drawn into a landscape that is wild and wonderful. There are those places that are difficult to reach that I would probably never have found and would unlikely to revisit if it were not for my pursuit of the fish that can be found there. The river Walkham flows off the southern slopes of Dartmoor and from Merrivale picks up speed as it drives down through rough pasture and unmanaged woods. Tumbling over boulders the size of small houses and through canopies of oak and rhododendron the little river creates a haven for all wild and living things.

In May the whole valley is carpeted with bluebells and with the first of the spring rains the sea trout come from the sea. The earliest run right through the river to take up residence in the deep pots above Ward Bridge about the same time that the bluebells flower. I make an annual pilgrimage and either park at Merrivale and work my way down or park at Woodtown and walk up. After over twenty years of doing this there remains a small section of the river in the middle that I have never fished and I doubt that anyone else during the same period has. I work my way up or down slowly, flicking a weighted nymph into the gullies and runs and twitching a dry fly over the glides. I will stop to watch a dipper feeding in the riffles or wagtails courting on the rocks. A kingfisher may dart past and a sparrowhawk sweep the glades. A day can pass me by and I find I have made little distance up the stream. The large silver sea trout that brought me to the valley are pursued with a passion but the setting absorbs much my fervour and softens any zeal. Time is lost as I meander with the stream and drink in its atmosphere. I catch a few brown trout and

DATE	RIVER	BEAT	CONDITIONS
June 2003	Tavy	Middle	Low Clear Full Moon 14C

NOTES

Fished Big Pool in difficult conditions with a low clear river and full moon. Succeeded in getting one fish from the shadows before the moon was high and another late on when it had dropped below the trees. When the moon was at its brightest I sat on the beach and enjoyed the tranquillity which was broken by a deer crashing through the undergrowth on the opposite bank. Above me on the high bank I had a clear view of a roe deer crashing out of the trees to cross the patch where the bank was too steep for trees to grow. How it had found its footing there I really cannot imagine.

FISH CAUGHT	2 sea trout 2lb 2 oz and 2 lb	FLY/LURE	Size 12 Black Special.

DATE	RIVER	BEAT	CONDITIONS
August 1999	Tavy	Lower	Low and clear

NOTES

Tried fishing at night on the top section of the Lower Beat. A beautiful night with bright stars and leaping fish. But it was new ground for me and I found myself trying to get the feel of the location as much as fishing.
The path from Murray's Corner runs along a steep bank by the side of a fast and noisy river. It is rutted with bullock tracks and is difficult enough in daylight. Negotiating it in the dark while trying not to use a torch proved challenging. While moving between pools I tripped over a badger. It 'frightened the life out of me' and I probably gave old Brock a shock.. After that I decided that it would probly be wise to use a torch. while moving around less familiar territory.

FISH CAUGHT	0	FLY/LURE	Size 10 Special

DATE	RIVER	BEAT	CONDITIONS
June 2003	Tavy	Middle	Low and clear 13 C

NOTES

While sitting at he top of the Run waiting for dark I became aware of movement in the water working its way towards me. Mink or otter? Suddenly an otter appeared on surface and appeared to be playing with something in the water. It climbed out onto the rock opposite me and I sat quietly to watch. It was carrying an eel about 50 cms in length and sat and ate it in front of me. Oblivious to my presence it consumed the eel and then continued its journey upstream.

FISH CAUGHT	2 sea trout 1 lb and 1lb 4oz.	FLY/LURE	Black Special 10

occasionally one of their migratory cousins but fish caught or lost has little significance when weighed against the whole experience.

I appreciate wild places and to walk alone by a river that crashes between moss covered boulders through woods of oak and holly is a great delight. To do so with a purpose, somehow adds to the experience. It focuses the mind and gives a direction to the expedition. The joy is that the goal is not so important that I am not inhibited from diverting from it from time to time to observe, explore, investigate or just stop and enjoy. A walk without a goal or purpose that just meandered aimlessly would not provide the same satisfaction.

I tend to set out to fish alone. Fishing can be a social activity and I enjoy joining friends on a boat for some sea fishing. On a boat you can enjoy conversation, banter and competition. On the river I often meet others and stop and exchange pleasantries and may break for some time in conversation but sea trout fishing is not a team sport and it is, at best, an activity for the lone hunter. A few times each year I agree to accompany a friend, perhaps a novice, someone new to the river or a club member who has had a run of bad luck and needs some encouragement. This is very enjoyable but for me, it is not real fishing. I get distracted by the talk and lose touch with the essential purpose. It is not through any meanness of spirit or dislike of company that I choose to fish alone. I am naturally gregarious and will readily join a party but when on the river I need to take in all the signs and signals without distractions. Without the intrusion of conversation and making the minimal noise I see and hear things that few others have been privileged to enjoy.

I know that from a safety point of view fishing alone may be unwise, especially at night but with some care and some precautions I willingly accept the risk. While I hope that others will emulate me and become other lone explorers

of the wild Devon valleys they are places with obvious dangers. It would be easy to fall, become injured and, if fishing on the edge of the moor, not be found for weeks. I urge those following me to exercise caution.

I always tell someone where I am going, where I intend to park and what time I will arrive back. I carry a mobile phone but signals are unreliable in the steep river valleys. If intending to fish the upper Walkham or other remote valleys I carry a whistle, a small bottle of water, a 'snack' bar and an emergency bivi bag in my fishing bag. If fishing above Merrivale or somewhere else on the open moor I also carry a compass. I know I could just follow the river if caught in a mist, but a compass helps to confirm directions. This practice arises from years of accompanying young people on walks across Dartmoor but it is not a bad habit and gives me a feeling of some responsibility.

My night fishing expeditions are now limited to the main pools on the lower river. A quick car journey followed by a short walk along rough but marked tracks and paths can reach these. I have not fished the wild pools on the upper river after dark for many years. Deeper into the moor there are no maintained tracks, no well-worn paths just the meandering and broken trails of deer and badger. It is difficult in daylight, almost impossible at night. Battling though untamed holly, blackthorn and scrub oak is hard enough when you can see where you are going. The trek back to the car when heading home becomes a testing journey and it is easy to get disorientated. Each stumble and slip underlines your vulnerability and although the experience is exhilarating, good sense dictates that it is not the right thing to do alone. Taking a companion would take away the magic and so I now only tackle the upper river in the daytime.

My fishing permit gives me an excuse to enter into this world and it grants me permission to enter onto what is often private property.

DATE	RIVER	BEAT	CONDITIONS
July 2004	Tavy	Abbey	Low clear 14 C

NOTES			
Fished through the night until dawn. When the first light hit the summer trees they became alive with birdsong. The fish began to move and I had a magic half hour with five fish hooked until the sun rose and began to break through the trees.			

FISH CAUGHT	2 sea trout 1lb 2oz and 1 lb 4 oz	FLY/LURE	Black special 10.

DATE	RIVER	BEAT	CONDITIONS
July 2002	Tavy	Middle	Low clear 17C

NOTES			
Heading downstream with intentions to fish Lower Dukes after dark I could see a large red/brown animal in the tail of the pool. Initially I thought it was a stray bullock or pony but as I got closer I could see it was a red deer hind. Fortunately I had a camera and crawled through the ferns to get a closer shot. It was walking in slow circles in the shallow water in the tail of the pool where I had anticipated raising a sea trout or two after dark. I was a little disappointed that my intended fishing had been disturbed but watching the elegant creature cool off in the late afternoon stream was a bonus. I sat amongst the bracken and watched it for some time before it waded out and melted into the trees.			

FISH CAUGHT	0	FLY/LURE	

DATE	RIVER	BEAT	CONDITIONS
July 1989	Walkham	Ward Bridge	Low clear and warm

NOTES			
Fished up stream of Ward Bridge at night. The Boundary Pool was alive with fish leaping and splashing. I must have hooked the smallest in the pool but it gave a good fight and I would have probably lost a bigger fish in the rhododendrons. About midnight a powerful scent filled the air and created a sense of exotic pleasure while standing by the rippling water. The fish stopped moving and the moon broke through the clouds, A magical time - miles from any habitation and deep in the heavily wooded valley I felt like the only human on the planet. Hooked two small browns which were quickly released and then reluctantly I left for home and bed.			

FISH CAUGHT	1 sea trout 1 lb 12 oz and 2 brown trout 6 and 8 oz.	FLY/LURE	Black Pennel 10

DATE	RIVER	BEAT	CONDITIONS
August 1988	Tavy	Middle	Low clear 12 C

NOTES

Had an enjoyable evening by the river with plenty of action. Two fish were landed but six lost. The ones that 'got away' became detached after a pull and a short upstream dash. I am not sure that I was completely focused as there was a lot of rustling in the tress surrounding me. I kept getting the feeling that something was moving in the dark behind me. I thought it may have been the bailiff who likes to sit back in the trees and watch through a night sight and so was not particularly worried, just distracted.

Once I had landed a brace of schoolies I decided to call it a night and as I turned away from the river to walk back up the path I tripped over a large animal. It let out a squeal and an angry snort before ploughing through the undergrowth. Momentarily I was terrified and put on a torch to see shaking ferns and perhaps the grey back of a badger. At my feet was a partly eaten fish – not mine but possibly someone else had lost their catch to Mr Brock.

FISH CAUGHT	2 sea trout 12oz and 10 oz	FLY/LURE	Size 10 Black special

The exclusion of the general public allows the wildlife to go about its business undisturbed and my intrusion seems barely noticed. The cost is rising and annually I wince at the pounds I have to pay for my club membership but at the end of the year when I review my season I usually feel it has been money well spent.

Some of my beats have unrestricted public access being part of the Dartmoor National Park. I try to choose my times and places for fishing these beats when the river is likely to be least populated. Early in the morning is a favourite time and in late spring the dawn chorus by the river as the first sunbeams dance upon the water beats any concert or firework display. Walking quietly by the water the quantity of wildlife never ceases to amaze me. Badgers trundle home after a night's foraging, foxes sniff along the tracks and roe deer nibble at the new shoots. If I am lucky I will get a sight of an otter or get close enough to see a heron spear small fish. The woods of oak and holly are alive with all manner of creatures during the first undisturbed hours of the day. All this seems to evaporate when the first dog walker arrives to shout after an errant hound or chatter with a partner. Somehow a single silent intruder is accepted by the wildlife. Perhaps it is the human voice or the noises of the pet but is surprising how a valley can seem bursting with life at one moment and devoid of it the moment someone speaks or a dog barks.

I would like the company of a dog and envy those who are accompanied by well-trained animals that sit obediently at heel. My family terrier alas is not so well schooled. She would want to wander and explore and I would be constantly calling her, she would be barking and the peace would be broken. When I am fishing she has to wait at home.

On many mornings I have stopped fishing and sat down to listen to the birds, watch the deer or enjoy the flowers in the early sunshine. Sitting quietly and without moving it is surprising how close birds and animals come. Deer do not seem to have great eyesight but have very acute hearing and I believe, a keen sense of smell. The sound of running water can drown out any sound I make and if I move slowly from a down wind position I am often able to get very close to feeding deer. Moving very gently when it's head is down feeding and freezing when it look up seems to work.

Roe deer can seem very stupid and will stand and stare at me if I keep still - only to spring away when I make any movement. The fallow deer in the Plym valley seem much more alert and I rarely see more than the rump bouncing through the bracken and brambles as they sense me before I see them. Occasionally I have met with red deer who can make horrendous roaring noises in the woods at dusk but are sometimes found cooling themselves in the summer streams. They are very timid and are difficult to get close to.

The evening and the following nightfall are other favourite times. Once all the walkers and day-trippers have gone home the river is left to the wildlife and a few fanatical fishermen. There is a special moment when the birds stop singing and for a short time everything is quiet. Then the bats come out and a nightjar may join them to float over the river. The stars begin to sparkle, owls start to hoot and the night has arrived. The still pools shake as the first fish move and the reflections of stars rock on the surface as the ripples from rising fish travel towards the bank.

Suddenly I become very aware of smells and the must of damp leaves and the greenness of crushed ferns fills my nostrils. In late July when the honeysuckle is in full flower the scent can be almost overwhelming, reaching a peak around midnight. At times I find I can feel almost intoxicated by the perfume as it wafts down the valley with the evening breeze. These

nights are very special and usually coincide with exceptional fishing activity.

In the dark, once the wind drops I find I can sometimes smell other humans before I see or hear them especially those who have a penchant for powerful aftershave or are smokers. One of the bailiffs likes to watch the river from the woods behind with his night sight. Once he has identified who is fishing is he rarely disturbs me but he takes great delight in subsequently telling me what he saw me do while I fished through the night! The embarrassments are just the tangles, trips, badly timed casts and lost fish but he seems note every mistake. When I smell cigarettes and I have seen no approaching lights I know who is watching me and I feel reassured, but I admit I take extra care.

At night sound becomes ever more important and I strain my ears to hear for my fly line falling on the water. Ripples and splashes help me locate rocks and moving fish. With senses heightened every sound is magnified and the muffled flaps of bats, owls and nightjars fill the sky. Badgers snuffle and snort along the bank and roe deer make short crashing runs through the woods. At times it gets pretty spooky and I understand people who feel uncomfortable in the dark and become worried by the noises. Sound becomes amplified by the peace and the rustle of a mouse or shrew can generate an image of something large and dangerous. There was a time when I switched on a torch to investigate some terrible beast bursting through the undergrowth to find a hedgehog grubbing for slugs amongst the dead leaves. On another occasion it was a roe deer trying to get through a bramble bush. Mostly I now stand still, and listen without flashing a light to see if I can identify the animal by sound alone. I have had one or two scares but so far everything I have encountered has been more frightened of me than I of them

The dark I enjoy and feel confident that there is nothing lurking with intent to do me harm. There are frequent claimed sightings of large cats on and around the West Country moors and I think that if they were present in any quantity I would see them on my fishing trips. There have been numerous occasions when I have spun quickly to see a dark form melt away into the words. Many a time I have stopped casting to listen to something padding across the stones. When leaving the river or walking between pools I have frequently heard movement and in the shadows I have imagined large dark felines following me. A clear sighting has defeated me and I have, as yet, been unable to confirm my stalker's identity.

Heading for home across moorland tracks in the early hours some strange shapes have sped through my lights but I have yet to be able to claim with any confidence I have seen 'The Beast'! These fleeting shapes seem too big for fox and too swift for badger. They could possibly be Munjac Deer or perhaps even wild boar but I am never sure. In some ways it is nice to be kept guessing.

It is hard to express how much I appreciate my sea trout fishing and value my access to a wild and untamed environment.s On my solo intrusions into the world of the sea trout I am able to travel back in time. immerse myself in an age old practice and indulge myself in the primitive impulses of the hunter gatherer.

I feel priviledged that I can continue the West Country peal fishing tradition. It is a quiet modest activity that serves the river well and puts something of value into the local communities. Like my forebears I take a few fish but my impact on the wild areas is minimal. I sometimes wonder how much longer this can continue. Human pressure on our deminishing wild places is increasing and this is having an effect. I hope that my notes, sketches and photographs will help to underscore what we have to lose.

The References

Although I do not quote directly in this collection of notes I wish to acknowledge the following publications. They have advised me in my approach to sea trout fishing and have influenced this compilation. I commend them to other sea trout fisherman .

Bluett, Jeffery, Sea Trout and Occasional Salmon, Cassell 1948.
This classic little book was written at a time when angling literature was still dominated by enthusiastic and learned amateurs It is full of truths.

**Dawson, Major Kenneth Salmon and Trout in Moorland Streams,
Herbert Jenkins, 1928.**
Some local knowledge and classic old photographs. Good tips for fishing association waters

**Dawson, Major Kenneth , Modern Salmon and Sea Trout Fishing,
Country Life, 1938.**
Rather dated tackle advice but read beyond.

**Falkus, Hugh, Sea Trout Fishing,
Witherby Ltd 1975**
I keep returning to this book and finding more in it.

**Joyce H. S. , A Trout Angler's Notebook,
Herbert Jenkins 1947**
Joyce regularly fished the night on one of my favourite pools, then hike two miles over the moors to catch the morning train into Plymouth - good history.

**Harris, Graeme and Morgan, Moc, Successful Sea Trout Angling,
Blandford Press 1989.**
Probably the best of the modern sea trout books. Highly recommended

**Wanless, Alexander The Science of Spinning for Salmon and Trout,
Jenkins Ltd 1946.**
Although the tackle has been updated the tactical advice is still relevent..

The Photographs

Most of the photographs have been taken by myself. Some of the 'self portraits' were shot with the aid of a remote control, others were taken by my daughter Kirry Colverson.

Page 1.
Heading for Double Waters from West Down - June

Page 2.
Landing a Small Peal - Hatchmill - July

Page 5.
The Chip Shop - Classic salmon pot and early sea trout pool on the Walkham.
'Nutting much about' but a fish in the bag!

Page 6.
The Green Punt - Appledore Quay

Page 8.
Appledore from Instow.
Fishing with my Grandfather.
The Sand Ridge at Low Tide. Memories of Appledore -

Page 10.
A Small Fishing Boat Leaves on Last of the Tide - as I did so often with my Grandfather.
A Good Brown Trout - one of my best from the Walkham on fly.

Page 12.
A Brown Trout on a Dry Fly.

Page 14.
Fishing the Upper Walkham Boundary Pool, May

Page 15.
Obsessed - Mad fishermen talk to themselves

Page 16.
Spinning on the Tavy

Additional information about the River Tavy and its sea trout fishing may be found on the Tavy Walkham and Plym Fishing Club web site.

http://twpfishing.net/

Printed and Bound by The Printing Press, Plymouth 01752 250580